HEALTHY MENTAL PEACE

LUIS FERNANDO RODRIGO
VALLEBONA

FREE YOURSELF

DISCLAIMER

CONTENTS

This book is dedicated to my wife and my children.

OPENING WORDS

Healthy peace of mind is not the absence of difficulties, but a wiser relationship with what life brings. This book proposes a practical path to cultivating an inner presence that distinguishes between what is within our control and what is not, and that allows us to respond with intention instead of reacting impulsively.

It is not about running from or denying the noise, but about anchoring our attention in the present moment, listening to our emotions without identifying with them, and maintaining habits that keep the mind and body in states of greater balance. Throughout these pages, clarity emerges from daily practice: conscious breathing, non-judgmental observation, and translating that awareness into actions consistent with our values and goals.

The foundation of this journey rests on three organically interwoven pillars: self-awareness as an internal map for identifying triggers and patterns; acceptance, which creates space to work with what arises without catastrophizing or denying reality; and a practical commitment to simple yet consistent habits that support mind and body.

From this triad emerge three core tools:

Conscious breathing to regulate physical arousal, compassionate observation to transform our relationship with emotions, and journaling or thought recording as a compass for clearer decision-making. Over time, these resources cease to be isolated techniques and become a way of life, available in any context: at home, at work, while commuting.

From there, the book explores three key elements that accompany the reader's evolution: consistency, patience, and curiosity. Consistency translates aspirations into daily micro-habits: a brief ritual upon waking, short breaks midday, and an evening review that leads to continuous learning.

Patience recognizes that real change happens at a human pace and that serenity is cultivated over time, not through shortcuts. Curiosity invites us to view each experience as a source of learning, to ask what message lies behind an emotion, and what internal resource can be activated to respond with greater clarity.

Across ten chapters, this book presents practices and case studies that shape a more conscious life: from identifying mental blocks and self-awareness to stress management, positive thinking, mindfulness, boundary setting, self-care, and gratitude; from emotional resilience to strategies for maintaining long-term peace of mind.

This is a project of care: for oneself and for relationships, an invitation to live with presence, empathy, and deliberate action. If you accept the challenge, you will discover that inner peace is not a prize reserved for a select few, but an everyday capacity that frees you to think, feel, and act with greater coherence and purpose.

ONE
INTRODUCTION TO PEACE OF MIND

When we talk about peace of mind, we're not talking about a complete absence of thoughts, but rather a different relationship with them. It's the clarity to distinguish between what is within our control and what is not, and the ability to respond with intention instead of reacting impulsively.

This state doesn't arrive overnight; it's cultivated through daily practice: conscious breathing, non-judgmental observation, and anchoring our attention in the present moment. By understanding that every emotion carries a message, we can process it without being overwhelmed. In this chapter, we explore the pillars of that inner peace: self-awareness, acceptance, and a practical commitment to healthy habits. As we move forward, we'll see how small, sustained changes can transform the quality of our lives, reducing mental noise and creating space for calm and focus.

Peace of mind isn't a distant destination, but a consistent practice that becomes an integral part of our existence.

The foundation of lasting inner peace lies not in denying challenges or eliminating all discomfort, but in how we relate to experience. By learning to distinguish between what is within our control and what is beyond it, we gain a framework for acting responsibly and serenely. In daily life, events often demand quick and necessary responses; however, how we choose to respond determines the degree of tranquility we can sustain.

This approach doesn't imply unrealistic serenity or indifference to circumstances; on the contrary, it involves the ability to sustain attention, examine our interpretations, and choose actions that align with our values and well-being goals. Therefore, the first step is to cultivate self-awareness: paying attention to our reactions, identifying what triggers tension, and recognizing the signals our body sends when mental noise increases.

Self-awareness functions like an internal map that helps us navigate life's waves without getting caught in them. It's not about endless self-analysis, but rather compassionate observation that allows us to recognize patterns without harsh judgment.

By practicing it, we begin to detect, with greater precision, which thoughts tend to anchor anxiety, which beliefs limit our actions, and which emotions recur in different contexts. A simple exercise to begin with is a brief review of daily experiences: stop, notice what happened, what it felt like physically, what thoughts arose, and what story we constructed around that event. This record doesn't seek blame but clarity, because when we name the experience, it loses some of its destabilizing power. Over time, self-awareness transforms into a kind of internal compass that guides both our decisions and our small, everyday actions.

Acceptance comes as a necessary complement to that clarity. Accepting doesn't mean resignation or complacency, but rather allowing emotions and thoughts to arise as they are, without the pressure to turn everything into a problem that must be solved immediately. When we accept, we reduce the resistance that tends to magnify discomfort.

This act of acceptance creates a space where the mind can work more calmly: it is no longer fighting against bodily sensations or the internal narratives that cloud its clarity. Accepting also involves a kind conversation with oneself: acknowledging vulnerability, validating the experience, and, at the same time, committing to action that promotes well-being.

In practice, this translates into allowing difficult emotions without catastrophizing, observing them with curiosity, and then deciding on a response that aligns with the goals of inner peace, instead of reacting impulsively to momentarily relieve tension.

A third fundamental pillar is a practical commitment to healthy habits. Understanding isn't enough; it's necessary to translate that understanding into routines that sustain the mind and body in states of greater balance. Here, the key is consistency and simplicity.

Small daily actions, repeated regularly, can have profound effects over time. For example, a brief mindfulness routine upon waking helps to start the day with conscious presence, a nightly review of the day's emotions facilitates learning what throws us off balance and releasing judgments that hinder clarity, and integrating simple relaxation or gentle movement practices throughout the day prevents the accumulation of tension.

All of this doesn't require drastic changes in life; it's about incorporating habits that, in their simplicity, support a more stable mind, more capable of sustaining attention and more available to those around us.

To understand how these pillars intertwine, consider a typical high-stress moment: a clash with a boss, an impending deadline, or unsettling news. In such circumstances, peace of mind doesn't consist of denying the discomfort, but rather applying the framework of self-awareness to first acknowledge the physical and emotional disturbance.

Then, acceptance comes into play by allowing this discomfort to exist without trying to suppress or over-rationalize it. Finally, practical commitment is activated: an action is chosen that, however small, keeps the course toward the goal of serenity. It might be a four-count deep breath to ground the body, a brief pause to reassess the narrative being constructed, and a concrete decision—perhaps delegating a task or reasonably postponing it—that immediately reduces the burden. This cycle, repeated regularly, transforms dynamics that once seemed inevitable into conscious choices.

Everyday experience, when applied consciously, reveals that peace of mind is not a static state, but a way of relating to life. It's not about escaping discomfort, but about engaging with circumstances from a clearer, more serene center.

This shift in relationship manifests in the way we breathe, the way we move, how we listen to others, and how quickly we regain our balance when something shakes us. In practice, inner peace becomes a kind of filter that allows us to distinguish between real needs and the false demands of our ego.

Therefore, growing in self-awareness, practicing acceptance, and maintaining healthy habits is not about perfection; it's a daily commitment to a version of ourselves that can respond with intention, even in the face of the inevitable.

A concrete example can help illustrate this framework. Imagine Marta, a professional facing a hectic morning with pending paperwork, an urgent email, and an interruption from a colleague. Instead of reacting with irritation, Marta takes several deep breaths and observes the sensations in her neck and shoulders that indicate tension.

She recognizes that some of this discomfort stems from an automatic belief that everything must be done immediately. She practices acceptance by telling herself that it's okay to feel pressure and that not everything depends on her. With this understanding, she decides on a practical action: she prioritizes tasks according to their impact and communicates a realistic deadline to her team for what requires collaboration.

Marta's experience doesn't erase the difficulty of the situation, but it transforms it into an opportunity to demonstrate clarity and self-respect, keeping the conversation constructive and reducing the likelihood of further burnout.

This type of response, repeated over time, strengthens confidence in the ability to handle challenging situations without losing composure.

The final reflection on this first topic reminds us that peace of mind is not an isolated goal, but a quality that can be naturally integrated into daily life. It is a practice that grows with consistency: each conscious breath, each moment of non-judgmental observation, each decision made from a place of greater clarity contributes to a serenity that transcends circumstances.

If we adopt these principles as part of our daily identity, we will discover that inner peace not only benefits the person cultivating it, but also their relationships, work, and overall health. A mind trained to respond, not react, is better able to sustain projects, truly listen to others, and hold emotions without letting them become overwhelming.

Ultimately, peace of mind is an act of care: for oneself and for others. It is a commitment to the present that translates into wiser decisions, greater presence, and a life that gradually approaches a coherent harmony between thought, emotion, and action. And if we repeat it patiently, this practice ceases to be a separate effort and becomes a way of life, a constant breath that accompanies each step and that, over time, reveals that true inner freedom lies in the ability to choose, again and again, the answer that nourishes peace.

The idea of lasting inner peace isn't based on the notion that life will cease to present challenges, but rather on how we cultivate a wiser relationship with each experience. This goal isn't about completely eliminating pain, uncertainty, or discomfort; on the contrary, it proposes maintaining enough clarity to respond intentionally when these circumstances arise.

> In this sense, perseverance, patience, and curiosity cease to be abstract virtues and become concrete tools that transform our daily experience.

Throughout the preceding pages, we've already outlined the foundation:

Peace of mind arises from a state of awareness that allows us to distinguish between what depends on us and what doesn't, and from the ability to respond rather than react impulsively.

This chapter turns our attention to the practical goal, to a serenity that isn't a destination, but a way of being in the world, sustained by simple habits that are maintained over time and, through repetition, become almost invisible, yet profoundly transformative.

Consistency is the first visible pillar of the peace we want to maintain throughout life. It's not about achieving great feats all at once, but about building a daily structure that, over time, strengthens the mind and body against stress.

The key lies in adopting simple, brief routines that, repeated each day, have a cumulative effect. It's easy to believe that emotional generosity or a boost of encouragement is enough to maintain calm, but daily experience teaches that emotional stability is forged through regularity.

Therefore, this part of the journey emphasizes creating micro-habits that integrate effortlessly into the daily schedule:

A short mindfulness session at the start of the day, a conscious pause mid-day, and a nightly review of the emotions that arise in response to the day's events. These practices, repeated as brief rituals, don't seek to suddenly change external life, but rather to recalibrate our internal relationship with what happens.

Patience, for its part, functions as the time that allows the quality of our response to be refined. In a culture of immediacy, it's natural to expect quick results; however, lasting inner peace requires an honest acknowledgment that emotional development has its own rhythm.

Accepting this rhythm means abandoning the temptation of shortcuts and miracles, and embracing a gradual process in which each small advance contributes to a more stable serenity as the weeks and months go by. Patience thrives on consistency and the absence of hasty judgments about ourselves and others.

When we perceive that improvements don't happen overnight, we can maintain the necessary discipline without falling into frustration, and this management of waiting transforms our relationship with our emotions: irritability, anxiety, or sadness no longer surprise us so much, because we learn to place them within a broader framework of growth and learning.

Curiosity acts as a driving force for continuous learning in the face of life's experiences. Instead of reacting to what destabilizes us, curiosity invites us to explore the message behind each emotion, what event triggered it, and what internal resources can be activated to respond more adaptively.

This attitude prevents paralysis in the face of adversity and, instead, transforms challenges into opportunities to better understand ourselves and others. Curiosity is not naiveté; it is a commitment to reality as it is, accompanied by the willingness to adjust our beliefs when evidence points in a healthier direction. Through curiosity, inner peace does not become resignation, but rather a compass that guides our decisions toward clarity, empathy, and conscious action.

> The combination of these three dimensions—consistency, patience, and curiosity—is supported by the pillars already established within the framework of inner peace: self-awareness, acceptance, and healthy habits.

Consistency, patience, and curiosity strengthen the ability to observe without judgment, to accept what arises without being overwhelmed by it, and to maintain daily practices that regulate the mind and body.

Thus, inner peace ceases to be an illusory state of "absence of problems" and becomes a robust way of living in the face of daily demands:

- A way of seeing, understanding, and acting that reduces mental noise,
- Improves emotional regulation, and facilitates decisions more aligned with our values and goals.

Let's consider, for a moment, a daily routine that illustrates this practical and realistic approach. Upon waking, dedicating five to ten minutes to mindful breathing and gently releasing bodily tension can make a significant difference in how we respond to the first news of the day or to morning demands.

Throughout the day, short one-minute pauses to bring our attention back to our bodies and breath act as anchors, preventing us from escalating our reactivity to setbacks or interruptions. During these moments, a mental check or brief journal entry can help identify patterns: what situations trigger irritability, what limiting beliefs are activated, and what simple adjustments can make the difference between an impulsive response and a considered one.

In the evening, a brief review of the emotions felt throughout the day and a deliberate exercise in releasing judgment allow us to end the day with a sense of closure and learning, rather than accumulated emotional exhaustion.

The central idea is that lasting inner peace is sustained through these everyday gestures, which do not require radical changes or a complete reorganization of life, but a gentle reorganization of attention and the relationship with experiences.

This approach has direct impacts on daily life: on the decisions we make when fatigue or pressure overwhelms us, on the quality of our relationships, and on our overall health. By cultivating consistency, patience, and curiosity, we strengthen a mindset that investigates rather than boasts; that listens rather than suppresses; that remains present rather than flees from discomfort.

The results aren't always miraculous overnight transformations, but they manifest as greater coherence between what we desire and what we do, as a freedom to choose responses that preserve personal dignity and respect for others.

Over time, this coherence creates a peace that doesn't depend on external circumstances, but rather on faithfulness to the process of caring for ourselves and the life we share with others.

CONCLUSION

Looking ahead, the central idea of this topic remains clear: lasting inner peace doesn't appear as a reward for overcoming a single challenge, but as the consequence of a sustained commitment to simple habits that strengthen the mind and emotional regulation.

It's not a goal achieved overnight, but a quality cultivated day after day, with patience and the curiosity that fuels the will to learn from every experience.

In the following pages, we will explore how to consolidate these practices within a practical framework compatible with the demands of contemporary life, always keeping in mind that inner peace is, above all, a way of relating to yourself and the world: present, conscious, and, above all, human.

TWO
IDENTIFYING MENTAL OBSTACLES

Sources of stress, anxiety, and negative thoughts emerge from multiple fronts in modern life: mounting work demands, looming deadlines, interpersonal conflicts that test patience, recurring financial worries, fear of the future that inflates every decision, and the inevitable comparison with others that erodes confidence. However, the root cause that most often bears the burden is not always external; it is our interpretation of these circumstances.

The same situations can generate very different responses depending on the story we tell ourselves about ourselves and the world around us. This chapter invites us to honestly examine these triggers, to recognize them without judgment, and to understand how they influence our breathing, muscle tension, and the quality of our decisions.

The first step, then, is not to fight against what is happening, but to learn to observe with detachment:

- To stop,
- Record what occurred,
- What we felt physically,
- What thoughts arose, and
- What meaning we attribute to the events.

This initial self-awareness, however small it may seem, already reduces the power of automatic thoughts and opens up a space to respond with intention instead of reacting impulsively.

When we look closely at these triggers, a crucial distinction emerges between what is within our control and what is not. External pressures may be real, but our response is largely mediated by our interpretation.

For example, an increasing workload might seem like an existential threat if the mind interprets it as lacking the capacity to handle it; or it might be seen as a challenge that, with organization and support, is manageable.

This difference in how we read the situation alters everything from our breathing to our muscle tension and, ultimately, the action we choose. Here, diaphragmatic breathing and basic thought restructuring cease to be isolated techniques and become tools that underpin every decision-making process. Conscious, slow, and deep breathing brings a sense of calm that facilitates clear thinking; thought restructuring, for its part, offers a practical way to shift our attention from catastrophic or absolutist interpretations to a more balanced and realistic understanding of the circumstances.

The recommended process isn't complex, but it is disciplined. First, conscious observation. When faced with a stressful episode or a thought that seems to repeat itself without resolution, it's helpful to pause for a few moments and internally describe three dimensions:

What exactly happened, what sensations arise in the body, and what thoughts cross the mind.

This record can be made mentally in a short time or in a dedicated notebook. The goal isn't to judge what you observe, but to map it accurately. By identifying patterns, such as the tendency to anticipate the worst outcome when someone doesn't respond immediately or the tendency to generalize a negative experience to all areas of life, clarity is gained. This clarity, in turn, slows down automatic responses and creates the groundwork for more adaptive responses.

Secondly, diaphragmatic breathing acts as a bridge between body and mind. When the body breathes shallowly or rapidly, the nervous system is activated, intensifying feelings of overwhelm. In contrast, incorporating deep, abdominal breathing activates the parasympathetic nervous system, facilitating the relaxation of tense muscles and reducing emotional reactivity.

A simple technique involves inhaling through the nose for a count of four, holding the breath briefly for a count of two, and exhaling through the nose or mouth for a count of six or eight, keeping the abdomen expanded during the exhalation.

Repeating this cycle for five to ten minutes regularly helps slow the heart rate, reduce stiffness in the neck and shoulders, and allow the mind to focus on what is relevant in the present moment, rather than dwelling on the fear of what might happen.

Basic thought restructuring is presented as a third operational pillar. It consists of identifying the automatic thought that arises in a stressful situation, questioning its validity by seeking supporting evidence, and, above all, formulating a more balanced and realistic alternative.

This exercise does not aim to deny emotions or invalidate the experience, but rather to offer an interpretation that allows for more effective action. A practical framework for practicing this involves three simple questions:

What evidence supports this thought?
What evidence contradicts it?
And what more balanced thought could replace the automatic one?

For example, when faced with the worry of presenting a complex report to a committee, the automatic thought might be: "If it's not perfect, I'll lose my credibility and my job."

Restructuring encourages considering: "I'm preparing this report with background information and reviews; I can present progress and ask for feedback to improve. If there are errors, I can correct them and learn for next time." This type of reframing reduces the likelihood of entering a rumination cycle and promotes smarter and more sustainable action.

Everyday life is full of moments that can trigger stress: a missed call, an email with a harsh tone, news that shakes our certainties. In each of these cases, mindful presence helps detect early signs of tension: a knot in the stomach, a clenched jaw, a thought that insists on an extreme solution.

Practicing presence involves remembering, amidst the rush, that the response can be crafted with the appropriate pause. Beyond techniques, it's about an attitude: the willingness to observe without judgment, to accurately name what is happening, and to differentiate between what is within our control and what is not.

This conceptual framework doesn't minimize the difficulty of the circumstances, but it does offer a way of interacting with them that preserves emotional integrity and facilitates decision-making under pressure.

To illustrate these ideas, let's consider the case of Laura, a professional who, during a particularly demanding week, felt anxiety cloud her judgment in critical meetings. Laura begins by taking a brief pause upon arriving at the office, breathing deeply, and noting three elements in her notebook:

The fact (several tasks with very tight deadlines), her physical reaction (tension in her shoulders and shortness of breath), and her thoughts (complaining about the lack of support and believing that any delay is a personal failing).

She then practices diaphragmatic breathing for five minutes and restructuring: she replaces the idea of "I won't be able to finish everything" with a more realistic one that acknowledges limitations, available resources, and the possibility of asking for specific help.

In the next meeting, Laura remains present, listens attentively, asks questions to clarify priorities, and proposes a concrete plan for distributing tasks. At the end of the day, she reflects on what she learned and records her insights in her thought journal. This small process, repeated throughout the week, transformed an experience of acute stress into a series of calmer and more effective decisions, with less emotional strain and a greater sense of control.

The consistent practice of observing triggers, coupled with simple regulation and cognitive restructuring techniques, doesn't promise to completely eliminate anxiety or negative thoughts, but it does reduce their impact on daily life.

Over time, the ability to distinguish between what is within our control and what is beyond it, and the skill to respond intentionally rather than react impulsively, become hallmarks of a coping style applicable to conflict, uncertainty, and constant change.

In this process, mindful breathing and thought restructuring cease to be isolated tools and become repeatable habits that sustain clarity, calm, and the capacity to act purposefully in the face of challenging circumstances.

If this framework resonates with you, the next section will expand on these ideas and provide practical strategies for continuing to train your observation skills and cultivate a repertoire of responses that promote peace of mind amidst the turbulence of daily life. Identifying mental obstacles isn't limited to an isolated exercise in introspection; it's enriched when we focus our attention on the everyday world where we live and make decisions.

Recognizing these obstacles in daily life requires sustained attention: during traffic, in meetings, when faced with news that stirs our emotions. It's not about a critical gaze or a collection of complaints, but about a conscious habit that allows us to distinguish, in real time, which parts of our experience depend on us and which don't.

It's at this intersection between what we can influence and what escapes our control that the possibility arises of responding with intention instead of reacting impulsively.

This chapter proposes a way of seeing that transforms irritation, haste, and uncertainty into data that can be analyzed and managed with simple and practical tools.

The essence of this approach lies in mindful observation: pausing briefly to notice what is happening, registering, without judgment, what occurred, what we felt, what we thought, and what we believe it means.

This act of pausing is not a flaw of modern life, but a deliberate choice that reduces the influence of automatic thoughts, those rapid chains that propel us toward maladaptive responses. When we learn to observe with some distance, without consuming our entire identity in each emotion, we recover a portion of the agency that haste often steals from us. Diaphragmatic breathing then emerges as a tangible ally: it is not a technique for escaping emotion, but a way to slow down the nervous system, stabilize the muscles, and regain clarity.

In an instant, the body ceases to be in "alarm" mode and enters a state of attentiveness that facilitates evaluation.

One of the core practices recommended within this framework is mindful breath counting. This involves becoming aware of the rhythm of your inhalation and exhalation, assigning a count that allows you to slow down the breathing process when tension arises.

For example, inhaling while mentally counting to four and exhaling while counting to four or six, depending on individual comfort.

This count is not a rigid goal, but rather an anchor that helps you distance yourself from immediate reactivity and enter what we call mental space: that broad lane between stimulus and action where we can choose the most appropriate response.

Alongside breath counting, a visual reminder can serve as a practical reminder of your guiding intention: a discreet note on your phone or a small sign on your desk that says, “Respond, don’t revolt.” This reminder acts as a bridge between intention and action, reminding us that emotion can exist without forcing us to act immediately in the direction its intensity dictates.

The mindful pause is another tool that integrates naturally into daily life. It's a brief interruption, one to two minutes, that allows you to evaluate possible alternative responses to a given situation. In moments of pressure, this pause can make the difference between a decision that reinforces balance and one that amplifies emotional turmoil. During this pause, you can consider different courses of action:

What would happen if I responded assertively
rather than impulsively?
What are the consequences of each alternative
for my goals and relationships?

This evaluation process doesn't seek to invalidate the emotion, but rather to enrich the decision with a broader and less rushed perspective.

Accompanying these practices with a brief thought journal facilitates the identification of patterns that might otherwise go unnoticed. The journal doesn't require lengthy entries; simply record, succinctly, what ideas arose, what beliefs remain active, and what scenarios repeat themselves in the mind in certain situations. Over time, this record becomes a map: it highlights recurring triggers, signs of burnout, and response tendencies.

For example, a pattern might emerge: faced with any minor conflict, the mind rushes to a negative conclusion, accompanied by a physical sensation of tension in the shoulders and neck. Identifying this pattern is the first step toward deliberately challenging it: next time, diaphragmatic breathing and conscious pausing will be activated before the mind jumps back to the thread of worry.

The power of this approach lies not in denying or suppressing emotion, but in facilitating a wiser relationship with what is experienced. When people begin to view their triggers objectively, a significant shift can occur in the quality of their decisions: less reactivity, a greater ability to assess potential consequences, and a higher likelihood of choosing responses that align with personal values and daily goals. In high-demand situations, such as a difficult meeting or news that generates uncertainty, the practice of non-judgmental observation and the use of a thought journal allow the mind to gain ground against the immediate stimulus.

This doesn't eliminate stress, but it does place it within a framework that doesn't dictate action on its own:

It's helpful to remember that the goal of these practices isn't to build a wall of silence around the mind, but rather to cultivate a more conscious relationship with inner experience. Mindful observation, diaphragmatic breathing, and basic thought restructuring work together to expand the range of choice.

> Instead of reacting automatically to irritation or frustration, you open yourself up to choosing a response that reduces tension, preserves dignity, and keeps you on course toward more sustainable outcomes.

This mindful approach is especially valuable because it's applied in daily life without requiring radical changes to your personal schedule.

It's not an isolated technique for specific moments; it's a way of being, a way of relating to your emotions and the external world that, with practice, becomes more habitual and less disruptive.

Over time, mindful awareness of triggers and responses has cumulative effects. Each observation, each journal entry, each brief pause reinforces the understanding that emotion is a signal that can guide, not a command that compels.

This gradual development tends to lessen reactivity and promote a more balanced state, even when external circumstances remain challenging. Daily life, with its varied rhythms and unexpected events, becomes a training ground where practicing sustained attention and self-compassion allows the mind to become accustomed to responding clearly, rather than reacting impulsively.

CONCLUSION

To conclude this journey, it's helpful to connect these practices with the next step in the book:

The deeper identification of mental obstacles and the coping strategies explored in the following chapter. Maintaining the practice of mindful observation as the foundation for identifying triggers and patterns is the cornerstone of this transition.

Regularly recording which triggers emerge and how they manifest in breathing, body tension, and decisions prepares the ground for moving toward more structured self-awareness techniques and expanding the repertoire of adaptive responses.

In practice, each day offers a new opportunity to observe, record, and choose; each conscious choice strengthens the ability to remain calm, even when the external world pushes in the opposite direction.

Thus, daily life ceases to be a silent battleground of emotions and threats and becomes an environment where the mind learns to collaborate with one's own well-being, and where serenity is the result of repeated attention and an inner guidance that knows when and how to respond.

THREE
SELF-KNOWLEDGE TECHNIQUES

Exploring emotions and mental patterns is presented as the gateway to self-knowledge and, at the same time, as a practical self-care discipline that transforms a person's relationship with their own inner world. This first topic of the chapter is proposed as an invitation to listen with curiosity, without judgment, to those signals that arise from the depths of experience.

Emotions should not be simply classified as positive or negative; they are, above all, internal communications that reveal needs, values, and boundaries that may not always be being addressed. By approaching them with an open attitude, we learn to distinguish between the valuable information they offer and the internal experience that, if taken as absolute truth, can disrupt our clarity.

This open perspective is not a relinquishment of responsibility; on the contrary, it is a way to gain room to maneuver, where the mind can observe without rigidly identifying with what it feels.

In this context, self-knowledge begins with the act of patiently listening to emotions without rushing to label them.

When we feel an emotion, whether it's physical tension, restlessness, or irritation, we can ask ourselves:

What need underlies this emotion?
What is my body, mind, or emotional system demanding at this moment?

Instead of reacting immediately, we can give the emotion a brief time to present itself, acknowledge its presence, and allow its message to surface without overwhelming us. This shift in our relationship with emotional experience, from reaction to observation, is the foundation of the emotional education proposed in this chapter.

The goal is not to suppress emotions, but to transform them into allies that guide wiser decisions, more aligned with our values and goals.

Therefore, curious listening involves recognizing that every emotion has a purpose:

To signal a need, a fear, an expectation, or a limitation that deserves conscious attention. As we become more familiar with this form of listening, mental patterns emerge that repeat themselves in similar situations.

Recurring thoughts, automatic responses to stress, and thinking preferences can become routines that operate in the background, conditioning our interpretations and, consequently, our actions.

This recognition is not intended to generate guilt or judgment, but rather clarity:

"This is a recurring pattern; this is how my mind tends to seek explanations; these are the beliefs that sustain this pattern."

Understanding these dynamics is a fundamental step in expanding the space between stimulus and response, between what happens and the deliberate choice of how to respond. Emotional anchors, those internal supports that sustain limiting beliefs, often take root in stories we tell ourselves about ourselves and the world. They can be ideas like "I am not enough," "I must please others to deserve love," or "Everything must be done perfectly to avoid conflict."

Identifying these stories and placing them within the framework of present experience allows us to question them more objectively and explore more realistic and useful alternative interpretations. This work is not mere introspection; it relies on concrete practices that help the mind gain autonomy from impulsiveness.

The heart of this topic lies in the practice of three simple tools, integrated into a brief but powerful routine: journaling, emotion logs, and intensity scales.

Journaling, or emotion diary, isn't meant to be an in-depth journaling exercise for every detail of the day, but rather a tool for mapping what arises at key moments. By recording brief notes about what happened, what emotions appeared, what thoughts accompanied them, and what beliefs tried to take hold, the individual creates a living map of their tendencies.

This map serves as a guide for identifying recurring triggers and understanding how those triggers influence breathing, muscle tension, and the quality of decisions. Intensity scales allow you to measure how strong an emotion was at a given moment, provide a reference point for observing changes over time, and facilitate the detection of patterns that might otherwise go unnoticed. Together, these tools help transform emotional experience into data that can be analyzed and used to take deliberate action.

Breathing, in this context, is not an isolated resource but a bridge between body and mind. Diaphragmatic breathing, slow and conscious, acts as a regulator of the nervous system; it relaxes tense muscles and creates a more favorable environment for observation.

When an acute emotion intensifies, simply pausing to breathe mindfully can restore the body and mind's equilibrium, reducing the urge for impulsive responses and allowing for a more considered reaction.

Mindful breath counting, for example, offers a tangible anchor: inhale to a count of four, exhale to a count of four, or adjust the count to a comfortable level. This exercise, repeated at intervals throughout the day, is not intended to abruptly eliminate tension, but rather to lessen its intensity and expand the window of conscious choice. In parallel, the visual reminder of the intention to respond—rather than to react—complements this practice, reminding us that autonomy in the face of emotions is cultivated with each pause and with each decision made from that pause.

The combination of mindful observation and the practices mentioned gradually shapes a habit that is not an isolated technique, but a way of life. Over time, the ability to objectively record what is happening, to accurately name emotions, and to distinguish between what is within one's control and what is not, strengthens.

This clarity translates into greater agency: the mind is no longer at the mercy of blind impulses, but can evaluate options, consider consequences, and choose a response that aligns with personal goals and values. This progress is neither linear nor immediate; it unfolds through a series of small advances that accumulate with consistent practice.

Each day offers a new opportunity to observe, record, and choose, and with this repetition, the capacity to maintain a more serene presence in the face of intense emotions, tensions, and daily dilemmas gradually expands.

In practical terms, daily life can be organized in a way that integrates these tools without creating an additional burden. It's suggested to begin with a brief moment of observation at the start, middle, and end of the day.

In the first hour of the morning, you can pause to identify a dominant emotion and jot down, in a few lines, what need it might be trying to address.

Midday, during a short break, you can count your breaths and check if any recent situation has revealed a recurring pattern. At night, the thought journal becomes a review that connects your experiences with beliefs that may have been reinforced.

> This framework doesn't require extensive time or full-time dedication; it consists of micro-practices that, when repeated, strengthen your capacity for self-control and conscious response.

A final reflection on this topic is that self-knowledge is not a static label placed on experience; it is a dynamic process nourished by continuous observation, the honesty to see patterns, and the courage to question beliefs that no longer serve us.

As a person learns to listen to their emotions with curiosity and map their thought patterns, a space of inner freedom opens up.

This space does not eliminate difficulties, but it transforms the relationship with them:

One gains decisiveness instead of being swept along by inertia, one gains dignity in one's response, and one cultivates a foundation of confidence that sustains serenity even when the external world presents challenges.

This chapter, therefore, lays the groundwork for the next level of intervention: self-knowledge techniques and coping strategies that will allow the individual not only to understand their emotions but also to actively shape their response to life's situations.

The journey, as has been said, is not a path towards an impossible perfection, but a route towards greater clarity, greater coherence between what one feels and what one does, and a life in which inner peace becomes a capacity that accompanies every daily decision.

Introspection and mindfulness exercises are practical tools for understanding our internal dynamics, comprehending the diverse responses that arise in the face of experiences, and training the mind to move more freely within daily life.

This journey doesn't aim to turn mindfulness into an isolated technique, but rather into a way of relating to oneself:

- A presence that observes,
- Names, and
- Accompanies without judgment, allowing what arises to present itself clearly and without trying to control the action.

Beginning with gentle attention to the breath, bodily sensations, and the thoughts that pass through the mind helps to detach the ego from each experience. It's not about denying the experience, but about viewing it with more distance so that the response can emerge with intention instead of being an automatic reflex. In practice, mindfulness arises from small, repeated moments of concentration throughout the day. Prolonged immersion isn't required to begin noticing changes: a few minutes of conscious breathing upon waking, a pause during tasks requiring concentration, and a brief reflection at the end of the day.

With repetition, the mind becomes accustomed to remaining present instead of wandering among thoughts that tend to repeat automatically.

This process doesn't aim to make the mind completely silent, but rather to create a state of greater inner stability where what is important becomes clearer and distractions lose their power.

The ability to observe without clinging is,
in this context, a core skill.

It involves naming what arises, acknowledging the emotion or thought that appears, and allowing the mind to settle without needing to immediately correct it.

This gradual recognition—emotion, physical sensation, mental image—creates a space between stimulus and response. In that interval, we can choose an action that aligns with our values and goals, rather than reacting impulsively to irritation, haste, or uncertainty.

It is a practice nourished by acceptance and curiosity: accepting what arises, without asserting it as definitive, and exploring what that experience needs to integrate more constructively.

Among the practices that enrich this process are brief mental retreats, pauses throughout the day to focus attention on the body and breath, and mindfulness interventions applied to daily tasks. A mental retreat, even a short one, can consist of spending ten minutes sitting in silence, observing the breath, noticing sensations in the hands, back, and neck, and observing which thoughts cross one's awareness without clinging to them.

These pauses don't aim to eliminate mental noise, but rather to learn to navigate it more calmly and with less tendency to identify with it. In daily life, mindfulness during an activity as simple as walking, eating, or writing can transform the experience: the pace slows, distractions decrease, and the ability to sustain attention is strengthened.

The fundamental goal is to cultivate a compassionate presence within ourselves, allowing us to respond calmly to life's changing circumstances. This compassion is not indulgence, but rather a way of sustaining ourselves in the face of the inevitable discomfort that sometimes accompanies the human experience.

Observing and caring for our own experience become tools for reducing emotional turmoil and increasing our capacity for concentration.

When we consistently pay attention, we learn to distinguish between what is within our control and what is not, and to position ourselves in a state of deliberate action rather than automatic reaction. This distinction is key to preventing emotional outbursts from dictating the course of our decisions.

Mindfulness practice and introspection also draw on paying attention to internal processes that often go unnoticed:

Beliefs that are repeated without being questioned, judgments that are triggered in certain situations, and mental habits that bring us closer to or further from what we call inner peace.

Through simple exercises, such as observing the breath during gentle counting, identifying physical sensations associated with emotions, or labeling thoughts that arise, we gain distance from the experience.

This distance doesn't imply distancing ourselves from ourselves, but rather accompanying the experience with a learning attitude.

It's about transforming the act of observing into a source of clarity that guides action more consciously, even when circumstances demand speed or complex responses.

A practical example can illustrate the potential of these practices. Imagine a professional who, in the middle of a tense meeting, feels her pulse quicken and confusing thoughts take hold in her mind.

Instead of reacting immediately with a defensive outburst or an emotional withdrawal, she recalls her mindfulness training: she breathes consciously, observes the sensations in her body, and labels the thought that arises—"this is a sign of tension; I want to respond clearly."

Then, she decides to take a short break, offers an objective summary of what was agreed upon, and provides an intervention based on facts, not on overwhelming emotion. After the meeting, she records her sensations, triggers, and chosen responses in a brief journal to identify future patterns and enrich her repertoire of conscious responses.

This type of scenario, without requiring long periods of stillness, illustrates how introspection and mindfulness practices can be integrated into work and personal life, strengthening the ability to cope with pressure without losing clarity or humanity.

Journaling, when used as a complement to other activities, can enhance the experience of introspection. Recording emotions, thoughts, and the situations that trigger them helps map patterns over time.

It's not about making writing an end in itself, but rather a tool for better understanding what activates certain responses and how chosen responses have affected outcomes.

Over time, this record transforms into a personal map of signals and strategies: what kinds of stimuli tend to generate intense reactions, what emotional resources are activated in moments of vulnerability, and what actions have proven most helpful in regaining calm and direction.

CONCLUSION

As we close this chapter, the focus remains on the possibility that every moment offers a new opportunity to practice mindfulness.

Cultivating inner peace doesn't depend on a state of constant tranquility; it begins with consistent practice and repetition to build a sustainable foundation. The intention is for the reader to feel supported in gradually incorporating these practices into their daily life, without unrealistic demands or unattainable promises.

Over time, compassionate presence ceases to be a distant goal and becomes a way of living: more mindful in every task, more patient in every interaction, and more resilient in the face of the challenges that inevitably arise.

This approach, in its apparent simplicity, offers a lasting path to a clearer mind, a kinder heart, and more intentional action in the face of life's circumstances.

FOUR
STRATEGIES FOR STRESS MANAGEMENT

Managing stress in daily life often begins with a simple yet powerful decision: to stop and use mindful breathing as an anchor to restore a sense of control to the body and mind.

In this vein, this section of the book offers a set of practical tools that can be used anytime, anywhere—from a boardroom to city traffic—to reduce physical tension, calm the mind, and maintain the clarity needed to respond intentionally to life's challenges.

Mindful breathing is not a luxury; it is a fundamental skill that specifically activates the parasympathetic nervous system, promotes muscle relaxation, and creates a space between stimulus and action—a space in which decisions become deliberate rather than impulsive.

Simultaneously, progressive muscle relaxation offers a quick way to release the physical tension associated with stress, reinforcing the sense of lightness and presence that the mind needs to function with precision. Imagine someone going through a particularly intense day: back-to-back meetings, endless calls, a barrage of weighty decisions, and a highly demanding atmosphere.

That person can begin with a brief pause for mindful breathing, a four-count exercise repeated three or four times, inhaling through the nose while counting to four and exhaling through the mouth while counting to four.

With each cycle, the toxin of haste dissolves a little more; the muscles in the jaw and shoulders relax, and the chest opens.

This simple ritual doesn't instantly eliminate external challenges, but it does change the physiology of the response to them. It is in this interval that the mind regains its grasp of reality: what is truly urgent, what can be postponed, and what requires precise action based on evidence, not fear.

The benefit is not only emotional; it is practical, as the returning clarity facilitates data gathering, the formulation of relevant questions, and the execution of a response that addresses both objectives and personal well-being.

Diaphragmatic breathing, performed with a conscious and comfortable rhythm, has a direct effect on emotional regulation.

As you inhale, the abdomen expands and the diaphragm descends, allowing for a fuller, slower intake of air; as you exhale, it facilitates the release of accumulated tension.

This pattern doesn't require complex technique or an ideal environment:

- Simply find a place to breathe,
- Even if it's in the bathroom,
- A hallway,
- Or during a brief break between tasks.

Over time, the practice integrates almost imperceptibly into your daily routine, so that when tension arises, your body automatically responds with longer, gentler breaths.

Add to this the practice of visualizing calm:

Xlose your eyes momentarily and imagine a place or experience that evokes serenity, whether it's a tranquil beach, a quiet forest, or a memory of a success achieved calmly. This image acts as a perceptual anchor that accompanies the breathing and facilitates a reduction in heart rate and muscle tension.

Progressive muscle relaxation, on the other hand, offers a short and effective protocol for deactivating tension before it accumulates in the body. It involves voluntarily tensing specific muscle groups for a few seconds and then mindfully releasing them, observing the sensation of release.

This procedure can be performed quickly, starting with the toes and gradually moving towards the head, or in reverse, depending on what feels most comfortable in each situation.

The valuable aspect is the experience of contraction and release, which breaks the chain of accumulated tension: the body perceives relaxation as a signal of safety, and the mind accompanies this shift with a clearer guide for action.

In combination with conscious breathing, progressive muscle relaxation fosters a holistic state of stillness that facilitates clarity, working memory, and the ability to apply practical solutions to current problems.

> The key to these techniques is consistency and adaptability. It's not about turning every stressful moment into a prolonged meditative experience, but about cultivating micro-pauses that become silent, reliable habits.

In real life, these practices should be adjusted to the rhythm of each day: at work, a brief pause between tasks; at home, a breath before responding to a family conflict; on the street, a sustained breath at a red light to prevent tension from building in the neck and shoulders.

With repetition, a kind of second nature develops: conscious breathing becomes the first response to a stressor, visualization of calm keeps the focus on the goal, and progressive muscle relaxation becomes a signature of tranquility that is especially evident when demands increase.

To illustrate the practical application, consider the following example: Marta, a project analyst, faces a high-level meeting where she must defend a strategic plan before demanding executives. The pressure is immediate: the room is filled with appraising eyes, and every word feels weighty.

At that moment, Marta employs a simple yet powerful sequence. She takes three deep breaths, focusing on the expansion of her abdomen and the controlled exhalation. On the third inhale, she incorporates a brief visualization of calm: she sees herself presenting data clearly, without distractions. Then, she initiates a brief progressive muscle relaxation protocol in her neck and shoulders to release accumulated tension.

With this physical and mental foundation, Marta continues her presentation with a calmer voice, states the data precisely, and answers questions with structured responses, without being swayed by emotional outbursts or aggressive interruptions. At the end, she pauses for a minute to notice her sensations and record in her mental journal the observed triggers and strategies used.

This record, which does not require much time, becomes a useful tool for adjusting future interventions and for reinforcing the ability to remain calm even in challenging situations.

Integrating these practices into daily life involves more than learning an isolated technique; it requires building a small arsenal of responses that can be activated in different scenarios. At work, for example, diaphragmatic breathing can become a brief ritual before a crucial meeting, preparing the mind to listen more objectively and to formulate valuable questions.

At home, a mindful pause between tasks can prevent the stress of a tiring day from spilling over into family interactions, protecting the emotional climate and the quality of decisions that need to be made together.

In moments of transition or emotional collapse, mindful breathing and progressive muscle relaxation act as practical lifelines, allowing us to stay focused on what truly matters and reduce the noise that clouds our judgment.

However, the effectiveness of these techniques depends on consistency: the mind strengthens when they are practiced repeatedly, even on days when energy seems low or the schedule forces improvisation.

The goal is for these practices to become part of a gentle routine, one that doesn't impose an additional burden but rather simplifies stress management. In this sense, it's advisable to set short, regular periods for practice, for example, a block of mindful breathing at the start of the day, a midday break, and a brief evening session to reflect and prepare for the next day.

The benefits aren't limited to a momentary reduction of tension:

Over time, the mind becomes accustomed to operating from a state of greater clarity, and daily decisions become more serene and evidence-based rather than driven by fleeting emotions.

This gradual transition to a way of being, rather than a goal to be achieved, is the essence of the peace of mind that is sustained by practical and sustainable habits. To conclude this practical section, it's helpful to remember that mindful breathing and progressive muscle relaxation aren't magic cures for external problems, but rather crucial tools for how we relate to them.

They are practices that strengthen our ability to observe, evaluate, and act intentionally, even when circumstances are challenging. By making these techniques habits, each person gradually gains mastery over their emotional response, a mastery that translates into greater coherence between what they think, feel, and do.

As breathing becomes a constant companion and progressive muscle relaxation a sign of self-care, daily life will find a more stable rhythm and a quality of action that reflects the inner clarity sought throughout these pages.

This foundation also lays the groundwork for the more subtle techniques of self-awareness and emotional management that follow in the subsequent sections: a bridge between the physiology of stress and the wisdom of mindful response.

Incorporating these practices into your daily routine isn't an isolated act of willpower, but rather a personal design process that transforms how you experience stress. It's not about immersing yourself in an endless list of exercises, but about creating moments, cues, and spaces that allow calm to emerge amidst activity, haste, and responsibilities.

In this sense, the key lies in structure and commitment: establishing a framework that allows breathing techniques, calm visualization, and progressive muscle relaxation to arise naturally when life accelerates, and not the other way around. This chapter, then, proposes a practical way to cultivate serenity without it seeming like an impossible luxury—a strategy that fits into a realistic schedule and adapts to different contexts, whether at the office, at home, or on the go.

Starting and ending your day with a brief ritual acts as a simple anchor, focusing your attention on well-being.

What might that be? A couple of minutes of mindful breathing upon waking to connect with your body and the sensations you bring from the night. A quick review of the emotions you experience while dealing with tasks and people, followed by a brief note of what you've learned or what needs adjusting.

This morning ritual, though brief, sets a tone: something you can rely on, something that doesn't depend on external conditions but on a conscious choice. Similarly, ending your day with a silent review of your emotions and a reflection on your responses reinforces the practice. It's in the repetition of these gestures that calm begins to become less fragile and more accessible, even when the environment is challenging.

Practical planning also involves incorporating simple reminders throughout the day. It's not about turning every minute into an obligation, but rather discreet inserts that, for example, schedule a 60-second pause to breathe and release tension.

These micro-intervals are humble yet powerful tools: they allow you to slow down, reconnect with your body, and reduce the intensity of your emotional response to an unexpected stimulus. In this context, the conscious use of pauses not only alleviates the immediate burden but also facilitates a clearer understanding of the available options.

A second form of support is creating a minimal physical space for calm: a corner of your home or a nook in the office with soft lighting, neutral colors, and an object that serves as a reminder to respond rather than react. You don't need to reinvent your entire environment; small adjustments that make the possibility of stopping and breathing visible when life pushes you forward are enough.

Gradual implementation is essential. Those who try to change habits without a reasonable plan often give up halfway through. Therefore, it's advisable to set realistic and achievable goals, such as a week of not taking on more than is truly manageable, or incorporating a five-minute breathing session in the morning and a two-minute break midday.

These milestones, simple in themselves, generate a sense of progress and strengthen confidence in the ability to sustain the practices over time. As people incorporate these routines, stress management transforms from a constant threat to a manageable state. The mind becomes quiet enough to see clearly, the body remains balanced, and the energy available for tasks grows, rather than evaporates.

The social environment and responsibilities also require conscious adjustment. Communicating needs and boundaries assertively is part of the self-care that sustains inner peace. It's not about chronically postponing obligations, but about prioritizing accurately and making it clear when a break is needed to prevent the load from becoming overwhelming.

This sometimes involves saying no to commitments that exceed personal capacity, asking for support when possible, and distributing tasks more equitably.

In practice, a person who manages stress effectively doesn't seek to eliminate difficulties entirely, but rather to maintain clarity in order to respond purposefully when challenges arise. In this context, breaks are not interruptions, but strategic tools that allow one to maintain direction and the quality of their decisions.

A key component of daily routine is, of course, paying attention to one's own internal experience. Here, a thought and emotion journal can become an ally. Taking a few minutes to record what triggers appeared, what beliefs were activated, what physical sensations accompanied the tension, and what responses were chosen, allows you to map recurring patterns.

This map acts like a compass:

It indicates when certain situations tend to trigger an automatic response and helps in designing more effective interventions in the future. It's not about judgment, but about evidence that supports sober decision-making.

To illustrate how these ideas materialize in everyday life, consider the case of a project manager facing crucial meetings with multiple stakeholders.

In one particularly tense meeting, she remembers to pause briefly to practice diaphragmatic breathing, counting to four on the inhale and four on the exhale.

With her body calm, she identifies the emerging emotion—a mixture of pressure and worry—and clearly states the objective fact: deadlines and quality standards are at stake. What could have been an impulsive reaction then transforms into a fact-based intervention: she presents accurate data, summarizes agreements reached, and proposes a concrete action plan.

After the meeting, she records in her journal the feelings she experienced, the triggers she identified, and the responses that proved most helpful. Over time, this record becomes a repository of strategies that facilitates faster and more effective responses to future stressful situations.

This practical approach doesn't deny the complexity of situations; it recognizes that stress is part of the human experience and that inner peace isn't a static state, but a skill that grows stronger with consistent practice.

Thus, daily routine becomes a laboratory for conscious responses:

Each day offers opportunities to practice, observe, and adjust. As these practices become automatic, the mind gains greater freedom of choice between stimulus and action; emotion ceases to dictate behavior entirely, and reflection takes its place between stimulus and response.

This interval, however small it may seem,
is the space where dignity is cultivated
in the face of adversity.

And that is the core of stress management in everyday life: not the absence of pressure, but the ability to maintain clarity, calm, and intention even when the environment is challenging.

CONCLUSION

Looking ahead, these daily integration guidelines pave the way for the next section of the book, where the power of positive thinking unfolds as an extension of stress management practices.

When these practices are consistent and relevant to each person's reality, the experience of inner peace is more easily sustained and extends to relationships, performance, and rest.

In short, incorporating these practices into daily life is, first and foremost, an act of care: caring for your attention, your body, your time, and your interactions. With this care, the ability to respond deliberately becomes a quality that accompanies every decision, and gradually, calm ceases to be a distant goal and becomes a constant presence in everyday life.

FIVE
THE IMPORTANCE OF POSITIVE THINKING

Cultivating an optimistic attitude isn't about denying reality or turning every obstacle into a happy story that avoids confronting discomfort. It's, first and foremost, a way of relating to what happens from a perspective that acknowledges difficulty without allowing it to define our identity or the direction of our actions. It's the ability to sustain hope grounded in experience and the evidence of our own capabilities.

This isn't simply about "positive thinking" as a mask; it's about building an internal narrative that supports the possibility of learning, adapting, and moving forward, even when circumstances are adverse. In this sense, cultivating an optimistic attitude involves three mutually reinforcing elements: realistic hope, active curiosity, and deliberate action.

These pillars are nourished by attentively listening to our inner voice, accepting our limitations, and having the patience to allow appropriate answers to emerge over time.

Realistic hope acts as a beacon, guiding decision-making when the path is unclear. It's not about expecting miracles, but about believing, based on past experiences, that there are possibilities for improvement and adjustment.

This hope is supported by personal evidence: small achievements, times we've overcome similar challenges, the feedback we receive from others, and the resources we've discovered along the way. Recognizing these signs isn't naive, but rather careful: asking ourselves what we learned from the experience, what tools were useful, and what changes we need to make to respond better next time.

This kind of hope prevents disillusionment when setbacks occur and ensures that motivation doesn't become a fleeting emotional state, but rather a practical commitment to realistic goals.

Curiosity, on the other hand, transforms difficulty into a learning laboratory. Instead of getting stuck in complaining or ruminating, curiosity invites us to ask:

What is this challenge trying to tell us?
What does the situation suggest about my habits,
my limitations, or my resources?

Curiosity doesn't erase the pain or minimize the effort, but it expands the possibility of seeing options that previously seemed invisible. Through it, difficulties cease to be tests that hold us back and become information that guides action.

In this framework, every setback becomes an opportunity to review our assumptions, adjust our strategies, and reinforce a growth mindset that, in the long run, strengthens inner peace.

Deliberate action is the natural culmination of hope and curiosity. Knowing what is possible, identifying what needs to be done, and then consistently carrying it out allows optimism to move beyond mere expectation and translate into tangible results.

Action can be as simple as reorganizing priorities, seeking support, breaking down a problem into manageable parts, or seeking additional information to make more informed decisions.

When action is framed within a clear direction and accompanied by a record of progress, the reader begins to notice that self-confidence doesn't depend on extraordinary luck, but rather on a pattern of responses that repeats itself over time.

This pattern is essential for maintaining peace of mind:

knowing that we can influence the course of our experiences
anchors the mind in a foundation of stability
and predictability, even in the face
of the unexpected.

To illustrate these ideas, let's consider a common workplace scenario: a team leader faces a significant delay on a key project. The initial announcement creates tension within the team and a drop in morale, but she chooses to respond with optimism.

First, she reviews the available evidence: what information exists about the causes of the delay, what progress has been made, and what resources are actually available. Based on this, she formulates realistic statements to guide the conversation and reduce anxiety:

"We have a delay, but we also have a clear path to catch up in the next two weeks if we adjust the plan and redistribute tasks."

This statement doesn't minimize the problem; it places it within a framework of concrete action. Next, she invites the team to share observations and potential solutions, fostering a curiosity that shifts the focus from complaining to building alternatives.

In this interaction, curiosity translates into open-ended questions:

What part of this challenge depends on us, and what part depends on external factors?

What small adjustments can make a tangible difference in the coming days?

This approach not only increases the likelihood of overcoming the obstacle, but also strengthens group cohesion by generating a shared sense of agency.

The cumulative effect of cultivating an optimistic attitude goes far beyond solving a single problem. In daily life, when reality is viewed through this lens, subtle yet significant changes begin to appear. People who practice a possibility-oriented mindset tend to react less to unpleasant news, maintain greater concentration, and sustain more positive relationships, even when tensions or disagreements arise.

This effect is not simply a matter of "default pleasant thinking"; it manifests as a way of managing uncertainty with clarity, avoiding catastrophic narratives that paralyze action, and cultivating a sense of continuity amidst change.

By incorporating habits that nurture this attitude, such as verifying beliefs with evidence, acknowledging small achievements, and engaging in conversations that foster growth, the reader strengthens their ability to maintain serenity without denying reality.

In practical terms, cultivating an optimistic attitude involves deliberately working with our inner voice. Realistic affirmations that we repeat daily, for example, should align with what we know and what we can validate with facts. It's not about denying difficulties, but about maintaining a narrative that allows us to envision the next viable course of action.

This creates a framework for continuous evaluation: what did we learn from what happened? What evidence confirms or contradicts our initial interpretation? What adjustments are necessary for the next decision-making process?.

This process of constant questioning and adjustment is, in itself, an exercise in emotional self-management that strengthens inner peace. The daily practice of this approach, even in small actions, anchors a way of being that remains stable amidst the instability of everyday life.

It's not necessary to turn optimism into a mask of invulnerability. Authenticity is a crucial component of the process:

Acknowledging pain, frustration, or fear when they arise, and, without denying those feelings, choosing to keep the inner dialogue solution-oriented. This authenticity is what sustains the coherence between what we think and what we do.

Furthermore, the environment either fosters or hinders this development: surrounding ourselves with stimuli that promote a growth mindset, such as readings that broaden horizons, conversations that expand perspectives, and practices that demonstrate the capacity for change, reinforces confidence in our own ability to transform reality.

Ultimately, optimistic thinking becomes the engine of inner peace when it is anchored in the truth of our experiences and in a commitment to our own well-being. It's not a static state, but a way of relating to life that makes it possible to respond calmly, serenely, and effectively to whatever the world presents us.

Practice, then, is not an ambiguous ritual, but a gentle discipline that adapts to each person. On days when stress hits hard, it's helpful to remember that optimism isn't about denying the weight of the situation, but about maintaining the conviction that we can act intelligently and compassionately.

On clearer days, this attitude fosters decisions more aligned with our values and long-term goals. If cultivated with honesty, personal evidence, and an openness to learning, optimism ceases to be a fleeting emotional state and becomes a way of life that sustains inner peace even when life is challenging.

We conclude this initial journey toward an optimistic attitude by understanding that, while reality will always present challenges, our relationship with them can be transformed. The goal is not to create a veil of unrealistic positivity, but to build a solid foundation for conscious action.

By nurturing realistic hope, stimulating curiosity, and committing to evidence-based action, we not only develop a mindset that facilitates navigating through storms, but we also strengthen the inner peace that is the foundation of Healthy Mental Peace.

This chapter thus lays the groundwork for the practical exercises that follow in the next section, where we will explore thought restructuring tools supported by this optimistic attitude, so that each reader can translate hope into concrete and sustainable steps.

Exercises for restructuring thoughts aim to deactivate automatic patterns that trigger anxiety or sadness, while simultaneously fostering a more balanced perspective on everyday situations. It's not about denying reality or cloaking it in a layer of improvised optimism, but rather about recognizing the influence of interpretation on our emotions and decisions.

In daily life, it's common for the same experience to generate very different reactions depending on the story we tell to justify it.

This chapter proposes a practical approach to intervening in that process, with simple tools that can be easily repeated and that, over time, cultivate a more stable foundation of realistic optimism.

The first course of action is recognizing the beliefs that are activated by each experience. In many stressful moments, an automatic thought arises almost automatically: "I won't be able to" when faced with a challenge, "I always fail" when confronted with a new task, or "it's not safe to take the risk" when faced with an opportunity.

These beliefs often don't originate in the present but are fueled by past experiences, learned biases, and an internal narrative that tends to exaggerate the danger or the potential for defeat.

> The result is an emotion that can cloud judgment and an action that, instead of being deliberate, is impulsive.

The first step, therefore, is to dare to listen to this internal dialogue without judgment, to notice when it arises and what evidence it provides to support it.

This act of observation is not simply recording; it is the gateway to reorganizing the situation, because only what is known can be questioned and changed.

Once a limiting belief is identified, the reframing technique involves evaluating the evidence that supports and contradicts it. This process has a simple yet powerful framework: pause to consider the information that supports the belief, look for objective facts and examples that challenge it, and, with these pieces in hand, formulate an alternative interpretation that is more realistic and useful for moving forward.

For example, faced with the idea of "I am not capable of defending my position in a meeting," evidence may emerge of past moments in which an idea was clearly defended, or of personal skills that have been valuable at work. From this evidence, a reformulation arises that does not deny the difficulty, but places the response in the realm of concrete action:

"I can present my points with clear data and request a review of the proposal, and if necessary, seek support from a colleague to strengthen my position."

This reframing is not a denial of complexity; it is a reorientation that transforms the energy of anxiety into a specific and feasible action.

In parallel, a gratitude and achievement journal serves as a practical tool to anchor the mind in the positive without creating distortions. This resource encourages you to briefly and regularly record situations in which you have achieved useful results, learned lessons, or made small progress. The idea is not to turn life into a catalog of accomplishments, but to create a record that reveals patterns of success and growth in the face of challenges.

By reviewing these entries, the reader observes that, even when circumstances remain demanding, there is tangible evidence of the ability to adapt, learn, and act with greater clarity. This habit reinforces confidence in the possibility of change, which, in subsequent situations, facilitates more serene decision-making and the more natural application of reframing.

Daily practice proposes brief blocks of mental transformation, designed to fit into a busy schedule. It is recommended to dedicate five to ten minutes each day to observing a recent situation, questioning the interpretation given to it, and reframing it in a way that maintains personal responsibility without exaggerating the risk.

These blocks can be integrated in different ways:

Upon waking, as a pause between tasks, or at the end of the day, as a review that completes the learning cycle.

The key lies in regularity and consistency. A revolution is not expected in a single day; rather, micro-actions are sought, small tests of change that, accumulated, strengthen the mind in the face of setbacks and stabilize a foundation of optimism that endures even when circumstances remain challenging.

Regarding micro-actions, the practical ground is enriched with tangible actions that delegate less power to emotion and more to informed action. Some of these actions might consist of drafting a realistic alternative to a limiting belief, practicing an evidence-based affirmation during internal dialogue, or verbalizing a clear solution proposal in the next meeting.

Other useful micro-actions include conducting a brief test of action, such as presenting verifiable data, requesting a review of a specific point, or proposing a pilot program to evaluate results. Repeating these micro-actions, within a context of patience and observation, will solidify the confidence that change is not only possible but also within reach in everyday life.

To illustrate the application of these ideas, imagine a professional who, before a meeting with a client, is overwhelmed by an automatic thought whispering that she doesn't have enough support to defend her position.

Instead of giving in to anxiety, she applies three simple steps:

- First, she identifies the emotion and the underlying belief;
- Second, she reframes the situation by verifying objective facts and finding evidence to support a more balanced perspective;
- Third, she proposes an action based on that evidence, such as presenting data, inviting a review of the proposal, and, if necessary, requesting support from a colleague to strengthen her presentation.

After the meeting, she records the triggers, beliefs, and chosen response in her thought journal, along with the observed outcome. This feedback records patterns that can be anticipated in future encounters and guides adjustments to improve her response in similar situations.

This example, while specific, reflects a common dynamic: the deliberate intervention in internal dialogue and the translation of that intervention into concrete actions that sustain a more stable emotional experience.

The promise of this practice is twofold. On the one hand, the mind is trained to distinguish between what is within one's control and what is not, reducing susceptibility to automatic thoughts and impulsive reactions. On the other hand, the ability to maintain a clear direction in the face of difficulties is strengthened. The expected result is greater serenity, increased clarity of thought, and greater consistency between what one feels, thinks, and does.

Over time, those who adopt these exercises will discover that thought, instead of being a source of inner turmoil, becomes a guiding tool: a compass that helps define goals, prioritize actions, and maintain connections to a broader vision of well-being. This path does not deny the complexity of life, but it offers a practical way to navigate it with intention and personal responsibility.

CONCLUSION

As we approach the end of this chapter, it's worth remembering that restructuring thoughts isn't a one-off trick, but an ongoing practice built on three pillars: honest identification of limiting beliefs, objective evaluation of the evidence, and the construction of actionable interpretations.

Consistent application of these tools, along with a gratitude and achievement journal, creates a constellation of habits that sustain inner peace even when external noise persists.

As the reader progresses, these practices will become part of a broader repertoire of strategies for approaching life with a growth mindset: a mind that observes without judgment, kindly questions its own narratives, and ultimately translates that questioning into actions that lead to a healthier and more purposeful daily experience.

SIX

MINDFULNESS AND MEDITATION

Mindfulness is presented as a path to calm the mind and reduce the noise that accompanies our daily lives. It is not a state of absolute stillness, but rather a more serene and deliberate relationship with the contents of experience: thoughts, emotions, bodily sensations, sounds, and the ebb and flow of the circumstances that surround us.

> Mindfulness invites us to observe without judgment, to remain present in our bodies and breath, and to allow whatever arises to pass without becoming a storm that sweeps us away.

This proposal, simple in its formulation, has effects that become visible with sustained practice: greater clarity in distinguishing what depends on us from what does not; a reduction in stress that allows us to respond with intention instead of reacting automatically; and a greater tolerance for discomfort, which makes it easier to get through difficult times without losing emotional cohesion.

To better understand the value of mindfulness, it's helpful to establish two central ideas. The first is that mindfulness doesn't deny reality or minimize difficulties: it acknowledges circumstances as they are and, from that acknowledgment, creates space to choose a response based on values and goals.

The second is that the experience of presence isn't an extraordinary achievement reserved for those who dedicate countless hours to meditation: it's a capacity that is strengthened through short, repeated episodes throughout the day.

In this chapter, we aim to explore, clearly and practically, what it means to be present in the here and now, how attention works when we train ourselves to direct it, and why daily repetition fosters a gradual but sustained transformation. The intention is that each reader can experience, within their everyday reality, the true experience of presence and take away a concrete guide to begin or maintain a daily practice.

The practical foundation of mindfulness lies in three simple yet powerfully effective movements. First, attention is directed toward the present experience without clinging to it or resisting what arises.

This recognition, which might seem like passivity, is actually an active act of observation that weakens the narratives we often tell ourselves about ourselves and the world. Second, the ability to observe with curiosity is cultivated, as if we were kind witnesses to our own sensations and thoughts.

This means allowing what arises to be present without immediately trying to control or deny it; instead, we name it, register it, and let it settle. Third, the separation between stimulus and response is practiced: there is an interval, however small, in which we choose how to act. This interval may seem minimal, but in practice, it becomes a space of freedom sufficient to align our actions with our principles.

The result of cultivating these habits isn't a promise that everything will be easy, but rather a stable ability to navigate complexity with greater clarity. In terms of benefits, mindfulness fosters a less scattered mind, improves emotional regulation, and provides greater tolerance for discomfort.

For example, in moments of pressure, it's possible to first recognize physical and emotional tension, observe it without judgment, and, based on that observation, decide whether it's appropriate to respond in a more focused way or whether it's better to postpone a decision until clarity has been gained.

On a practical level, mindfulness offers short, regular sessions that can be adapted to any schedule:

In the morning upon waking, during brief breaks at work, or at night as part of a wind-down routine for rest.

Short sessions are considered, within this framework, realistic and accessible tools for change. A typical practice might consist of five to ten minutes of focused breathing upon waking. This involves noticing the air entering and leaving the body, the sensation in the chest or abdomen as you breathe, and any thoughts that arise without trying to suppress them.

A second step involves a brief body scan: slowly directing your attention from the crown of your head to the soles of your feet, registering any tension or sensations without immediately trying to change them.

Over time, these simple practices can be expanded to include attentive listening to ambient sounds or observing bodily sensations during a mindful walk.

The key lies in consistency and maintaining a kind of curious attitude toward your own experience, without demanding perfection.

To illustrate the applicability of these ideas, let's consider a practical example of someone working in a high-pressure corporate environment. On a morning marked by the rush and pressure of a crucial meeting, they decide to take a brief mindfulness break before entering.

They sit in a chair, close their eyes, and focus their attention on their breath, counting four breaths in and four breaths out. With each cycle, they notice the rise and fall of tension in their shoulders and neck and recognize that some of that tension is a response to anticipating the discussion.

After two minutes, they focus on the body to filter out the sensations of a stiff neck, tense hands, and shallower breathing. Once the body has bridged the gap to calm, the person opens their eyes, breathes again, and, with a clearer mind, mentally reviews the relevant facts of the meeting: objective data, deadlines, and potential evidence-based solutions.

During the discussion, they continue to remind themselves of the intention to respond clearly rather than react to momentary emotion. At the end, you can briefly record in a notebook or on a digital note

what triggers appeared, what emotions arose, and what responses proved effective. This type of practice is not intended to eliminate tension, but rather to manage it with greater serenity and an emphasis on deliberate action.

This chapter opens the door to deeper exploration in the following sections, where we will examine mindfulness techniques and their integration into daily life in greater detail.

The aim is that, building upon these foundations, the reader will develop an ongoing relationship with presence:

A presence that doesn't deny difficulty but transforms it into a field of learning and conscious action. Repetition is key to this path. Each session, however brief, contributes to a practice that gradually shifts automatic functioning toward more effective responses, aligned with the values one wishes to uphold. Presence is not an isolated state; it is a way of being in the world that thrives on patience, consistency, and curiosity.

Therefore, as we conclude this first topic, the invitation is simple yet powerful:

- Begin with what is feasible today,
- With a brief mindfulness session, and
- Let the experience speak for itself, discovering how the mind can become a more stable ally in the face of daily challenges.

In short, mindfulness and meditation offer a practical framework for cultivating a calm that is not passive, but active and purposeful. It's about investing in a presence that allows us to distinguish what depends on us and what doesn't, so that every decision, every interaction, and every daily task can be done with greater clarity and a more solid foundation of intention.

This first chapter of Mindfulness and Meditation doesn't aim to present an exhaustive doctrine, but rather to offer a usable guide:

An invitation to experience, with humility and consistency, the true experience of presence. As you progress, you can adapt the practices to your own pace and context, validating the impact on your own well-being, your ability to concentrate, and your capacity to respond with dignity to whatever life presents.

The daily practice of mindfulness and meditation is proposed as an accessible path to sustaining presence and reducing the mental noise that accompanies our days. It's not about reaching a state of absolute stillness immediately, but about cultivating a constant relationship with attention: a presence that observes, accompanies, and then acts from a place of greater clarity.

This approach adapts to modern life, allowing continuity not to depend on large blocks of time or perfect conditions, but on the regularity of small moments that, added together, strengthen both mind and body. The guide offered here aims to transform this practice into a practical habit, easy to incorporate into existing routines, whether at home, in the office, or outdoors.

The goal is for each person to experience, through simple exercises, what it means to be present, not to try to revolutionize the experience immediately, but little by little, one session after another.

Beginning a daily practice involves understanding what obstacles may arise and how to address them with kindness. The first step is accepting that attention tends to wander, that the mind seeks distractions, and that the body may resist silence or stillness. Within this framework, the first short session, lasting five to ten minutes, becomes a gentle exploration: sit at the appropriate height, maintain a comfortable yet alert posture, and choose to keep a soft gaze, closing your eyes or looking down to reduce visual stimuli.

Take the breath as your primary anchor: breathe naturally, without forcing it, and count by fours or sixes, depending on your comfort level. The goal is not to "control" the mind, but to train it to gently return each time it wanders.

When the mind does wander—and it will—the instruction is simple and effective: return your attention to the breath, without judgment, with an attitude of gentle curiosity. Over time, this consistent repetition ceases to feel like an effort and becomes a state of presence that accompanies your daily experience.

Then there's the midday break, a brief window to restore clarity amidst the demands of the day. This break can last between one and two minutes, and its practical format is very clear: stop, breathe consciously, feel your body, and register, if possible, what arises in that moment.

At that moment, the intention to respond takes precedence over impulsiveness; a brief mental decision is made about how to act in a specific situation, be it a meeting, a conversation, or a task that requires concentration. Although it may seem minimal, this midday breath acts as an anchor that allows attention to refocus and responses to align with personal values and objectives. If someone prefers, they can accompany the break with a brief observation of three senses: what they hear, what they feel in their body, and what they perceive in their surroundings at that moment. This simplicity may seem modest, but it acts as a point of return when the day accelerates.

Finally, the evening reflection closes the daily cycle with a compassionate look back at what has transpired.

In just a few minutes, you can review the day's experience: which moments demanded greater presence, which interruptions interfered with your focus, and which strategies worked to regain calm.

This closing isn't about labeling the day as "good" or "bad," but rather about extracting practical lessons: which techniques helped maintain serenity, which distractions reappear, and what simple adjustments can facilitate the next scenario.

If this closing is accompanied by a brief note of intention for the following day, the practice transforms into a living project, focused on continuity rather than perfection.

For this guide to be useful, it's helpful to present three core ideas that strengthen adherence.

1. Regularity is more powerful than duration. A consistent, even brief, session creates a gradual change that is noticeable in both mental clarity and emotional regulation.
2. Acceptance is key: an ideal state isn't required at every moment, but rather the ability to return to focus after each distraction with an attitude of understanding, not self-criticism.
3. Gentle curiosity is the fuel: every experience, including distraction, becomes valuable information about one's own attention and what one manages best.

In terms of practical structure, the proposal is flexible and adaptable to different lifestyles. Those with more time can extend the morning session to ten minutes, maintaining the same sequence of breath observation, body awareness, and thought exploration.

Those who already have a particularly hectic day can adjust to a shorter version without losing the essence: a couple of minutes of conscious breathing upon waking and a minute for a mindful pause at some point during the day.

In all cases, the key is maintaining an attitude of openness and curiosity toward whatever arises. It's not about forcing a state of tranquility, but about creating conditions in which calm can blossom naturally when given space and time.

Everyday experience offers real-life scenarios where this guidance can come to life. Imagine a professional arriving at the office and, before turning on her computer, conducting a five-minute mini-session: she breathes, notices the sensations in her chest and hands, observes if thoughts of pressure or worry arise, and then sets an intention for the day, such as "respond clearly and seek evidence before making judgments."

Later, during a lunch break, she might repeat a cycle of gentle breathing, remembering that she is returning to presence, and conclude with a brief mental review of how a recent encounter was resolved by maintaining attention in the present moment.

At home, at the end of the day, she might engage in a mindful discussion with a family member, taking one to three minutes to return to her body and breath, identifying emotions, and choosing an action based on shared facts and values.

These examples illustrate that the practice is not an additional burden, but rather a restructuring of how we interact with time, people, and tasks.

Building on this foundation, it's important to remember that the experience of mindfulness and meditation isn't simply a matter of isolated techniques. It is, above all, a continuous relationship with one's own attention, a way of being in the world that fosters deliberate responses rather than automatic reactions.

The key lies in maintaining regular practice with an attitude of acceptance, recognizing that the mind tends to wander and that unpredictable days will require simple, realistic adjustments.

As individuals become more familiar with the daily rhythm, the sessions cease to feel like a separate exercise and begin to integrate into everyday life: walking, working, conversations, resting.

In this sense, the guide to starting a daily practice doesn't propose an unattainable goal, but rather a sustainable path that encourages continuity and personal growth through small, yet consistent, acts of mindfulness.

CONCLUSION

In short, a daily practice of mindfulness and meditation, when approached with humility and patience, can become a reliable ally against the fast pace and noise of modern life. It is not a static refuge, but a way of being present that enhances clarity, reduces reactivity, and creates space for responses more aligned with personal values and goals.

The key lies in consistency: five to ten minutes in the morning, a brief pause at midday, and a light reflection at the end of the day, all accompanied by a gentle curiosity that transforms each experience into a learning opportunity.

Within this framework, daily practice ceases to be an extra task and becomes a way of life that sustains inner peace, even as the outside world continues to move at breakneck speed.

SEVEN
SETTING BOUNDARIES AND SELF-CARE

Setting healthy boundaries is an act of self-care that protects energy and focus, but it's also a way to express self-respect and respect for others. In everyday life, from personal relationships to professional ones and family responsibilities, the ability to define what is acceptable and what is not makes all the difference between a day navigating with clarity and one where burnout, irritability, and a feeling of having lost control take center stage. Boundaries aren't rigid walls that isolate us, but rather tools that allow us to prioritize what truly matters, avoid unnecessary commitments, and conserve energy for what sustains our well-being, our decisions, and our connections.

By understanding that everyone has a different threshold, we learn to design boundaries that work for each context, without falling into extremes that hinder collaboration or turn daily life into a series of sacrifices.

The key lies in understanding that boundaries are a two-way street. It's not about unilaterally imposing restrictions, but about communicating needs, expectations, and available time clearly, empathetically, and assertively.

To the extent that we are able to explicitly express what we need to perform effectively, we give others the opportunity to respond more efficiently. This involves, on the one hand, recognizing our own priorities and, on the other, learning to manage the responses of those around us.

When someone perceives their boundaries not as a personal affront but as a guide for better collaboration, the likelihood of conflict decreases, and more conducive conditions for constructive dialogue emerge. In this context, consistency and patience become allies.

Coherence in words and actions strengthens trust, and patience allows for adjusting boundaries as circumstances change without losing sight of the central goal:

Protecting inner peace and maintaining
the ability to contribute sustainably.

A central part of this chapter is precisely understanding what boundaries we need in different areas. In personal relationships, there may be limits on emotional availability, time spent together, or the intensity of interaction.

In the workplace, boundaries are usually related to workload, business capacity, and the need for concentration on tasks that require focus; it also touches on aspects such as constant interruptions, the need for meetings with clear agendas, and the importance of preserving time for deep work.

In the family, boundaries relate to the organization of responsibilities, the use of shared space, expectations regarding mutual support, and the distribution of household chores.

Recognizing these dimensions helps to create a realistic map of what we can and cannot give, how we communicate this, and how we negotiate to ensure that the decisions made are sustainable over time.

Effectively communicating boundaries requires simple yet powerful tools. First, emotional clarity and precision in language: expressing not only what you don't want to do, but also why it's necessary and how it impacts your own performance and well-being. This helps avoid ambiguous justifications that fuel resistance or misunderstanding.

Second, assertiveness as an interaction style that defends your rights without infringing on the rights of others. Assertiveness is not confrontation, but an honest expression of needs, accompanied by explicit respect for the needs of others. Third, empathy as a bridge that facilitates agreement: understanding why someone might need more or less of your presence or availability can open doors to alternatives that work for everyone.

Finally, sustained consistency over time: a one-off conversation isn't enough; boundaries must be maintained in daily practice, adjusting them when necessary and, above all, ensuring coherence between what is said and what is done.

To turn these ideas into concrete habits, it's helpful to think of boundaries as a structure that can begin with simple actions and then evolve. A first step is identifying personal boundaries that, if crossed, affect emotional balance or performance.

This process usually requires honesty with oneself: recognizing which situations produce fatigue, irritability, or a loss of focus, and then deciding what practical changes are feasible without creating more tension.

Next comes the communication stage: choosing the right time to talk, phrasing the request with language that describes observable behaviors rather than judgments about people, and proposing alternatives that keep the course toward shared goals.

At this point, gradual implementation becomes crucial. Instead of suddenly imposing a new way of working or living together, small adjustments can be tested, their effect evaluated, and what works consolidated. This approach reduces resistance and increases the likelihood that boundaries will become a natural part of the routine.

An example illustrating this process can help to understand the practical scope of these principles. Imagine Laura, a project professional who, for months, repeatedly accepted extra tasks to avoid "looking bad" in front of her team. Over time, the excessive commitments began to affect her performance and her ability to focus on the tasks that mattered most.

Laura decided, honestly and carefully, to communicate to her manager the need to establish clear boundaries: she agreed on a work schedule that allowed for blocks of time for in-depth work, set a reasonable maximum number of tasks per week, and proposed a system for reviewing team priorities to avoid backlogs. She also participated in the distribution of responsibilities within the team to ensure a more equitable workload.

The result was improved quality of deliverables, fewer inappropriate interruptions, and a more trusting relationship between Laura and her manager, based on empathetic communication and the recognition of boundaries as essential for sustainability.

In other contexts, boundaries are expressed in more intimate spheres, such as the need for personal time to recharge. For example, a couple might agree on specific times to dedicate to their relationship, as well as separate times for individual projects or rest.

In parenting, boundaries help teach children that caring for their own well-being also requires limits on the attention they receive from others. In each case, the key is reciprocity: when boundaries are respected, cooperation is facilitated, and accumulated fatigue, which erodes trust and clarity of intention, is avoided.

It's important to recognize that setting boundaries isn't without its challenges. There are times when those close to you may feel insecure or even resentful about changes, or they may interpret a refusal as rejection. In these situations, it's helpful to revisit the conversation with language that emphasizes the benefits for everyone: greater efficiency at work, fewer conflicts, greater clarity on shared priorities, and ultimately, a life where available energy is applied to what truly matters. The temptation to give in to social or professional pressure to avoid conflict may also arise; here, practicing self-compassion is crucial: remembering that caring for yourself isn't selfish, but rather the foundation for being able to better care for others. Patience and repetition are key allies in building boundaries that will have the strength to withstand resistance.

With firm boundaries comes a sense of stability that benefits not only the individual but also their environment. Workspaces become more predictable, relationships gain authenticity, and decisions are made with greater serenity.

The peace of mind we seek is not based on denying life's demands, but on the ability to decide, at any given moment, what deserves our attention and how much we are willing to give.

This chapter, by emphasizing the need for healthy boundaries and self-care, proposes understanding boundaries as a frontier of growth: a diagonal path forward that preserves the energy to act with intention, build relationships based on mutual respect, and maintain a sense of purpose that is not diluted by external pressure.

Ultimately, setting boundaries is not an isolated act, but a habit that is strengthened through daily practice and consistency between what we believe and what we do. It is an act of responsibility toward oneself and others: a conscious decision to invest in clarity, calm, and dignity. By integrating these principles, the reader not only protects their peace of mind but also creates the conditions for daily life, with its varying demands, to unfold from a place of greater freedom, responsibility, and inner peace. This framework of boundaries and self-care will naturally pave the way for further reflections on how to care for oneself while still appreciating and responding to the needs of others, always guided by consistency between values, actions, and relationships.

Self-care is not a luxury or a whim, but the concrete foundation upon which the peace of mind of anyone seeking to maintain their clarity, energy, and empathy over time rests.

Small daily actions can make a significant difference when they become sustainable habits. Developing a daily relationship with self-care allows the mind the necessary space to respond calmly to situations, instead of reacting from fatigue, urgency, or overload.

This approach does not minimize responsibilities or challenges; on the contrary, it strengthens the ability to face these realities with greater balance, discernment, and presence. In this chapter, we explore simple practices that anyone can incorporate without overwhelming their schedule, with the conviction that self-care is, indeed, the foundation of inner peace that manifests in the body, in decisions, and in the quality of relationships.

Among the actions that comprise self-care, five fundamental pillars stand out: adequate rest, mindful eating, regular movement, time for creativity, and connection with people who inspire tranquility.

Each of these dimensions nurtures emotional resilience and the ability to respond to challenges with a calmness that doesn't depend on external circumstances.

Adequate rest isn't simply about sleeping more; it's about recognizing when the body and mind need to slow down and allowing recovery to occur with dignity. Mindful eating involves listening to the body's signals, choosing foods that sustain stable energy throughout the day, and avoiding peaks that generate irritability or lethargy.

Regular movement isn't about achieving competitive goals, but rather about maintaining physical mobility and the flow of emotional energy; a short walk, gentle stretching, or a mobility session can radically change one's mental state.

Time for creativity is an investment in inner vitality: a moment to explore, enjoy a hobby, or give shape to ideas that fuel curiosity and a sense of accomplishment. And the connection with people who inspire tranquility acts as a social anchor: conversing, sharing moments of support and receiving empathetic feedback strengthen the sense of belonging and reduce the feeling of isolation in the face of difficulties.

To make these practices a natural part of daily life, it's helpful to translate them into simple and sustainable rituals. A brief morning ritual can last between five and ten minutes: drink a glass of water, take a short walk or do some gentle stretches to awaken the body, and dedicate a few minutes to setting a clear intention for the day.

This focused start promotes a presence that lasts beyond the first task, influencing how we choose to approach the rest of our activities. In the middle of the day, short moments of mindful pause, one to two minutes, allow us to stop, notice bodily sensations, and recalibrate our attention.

During these pauses, it's helpful to remember the purpose of responding with intention and not merely reacting to pressure. At the end of the day, a brief silence or a gratitude practice can close the cycle with a sense of closure and balance, allowing us to continue tomorrow with renewed focus. Essentially, it's about designing the day so that self-care isn't an isolated event, but a structure that sustains calm and fosters clarity.

The consistent practice of self-care is also deeply connected to establishing healthy boundaries.

When a person takes care of themselves, the ability to say "no" to commitments that exceed their capacity to sustain them without burnout emerges more easily. This connection is not understood as selfishness, but as an act of responsibility toward oneself and others: by taking care of yourself, you can give your best without compromising your long-term health.

In practice, this translates into planning the day in advance, identifying which demands can be postponed or delegated, and, when appropriate, asking for support or adjusting expectations.

The energy saved through well-managed self-care is transformed into emotional availability for loved ones and for tasks that require greater concentration and creativity.

Self-care also strengthens the ability to respond to challenges with serenity. When demands increase, the temptation to react impulsively tends to grow. However, an individual who has cultivated habits of rest, nutrition, and exercise, as well as moments of creativity and connection, has a higher threshold for tolerating discomfort. This tolerance doesn't mean avoiding discomfort, but rather navigating it with an internal strategy that prioritizes presence and reasoning.

In practice, this means that when faced with criticism, a tight deadline, or unexpected news, the person can pause, evaluate the available options, and choose a response aligned with their values and goals, instead of giving in to defensive impulses or passive resignation.

> The result is a life with more available energy, fewer impulsive reactions, and a more stable inner peace that is reflected in every area: work, relationships, and sleep.

To illustrate this dynamic, let's consider the case of Claudia, a team leader who has decided to make self-care a priority.

Claudia begins by incorporating a brief, ten-minute morning ritual: she starts her day with a glass of water, does some light stretching, and writes down three things she hopes to accomplish that day, accompanied by a quick observation of her emotional state.

Throughout the day, she sets aside two one-minute micro-pauses to breathe and anchor her attention, allowing her inner gaze to witness any tension that arises and reminding herself that she can choose to respond with intention.

At lunch, Claudia practices mindful eating, savoring each bite and noticing satiety cues that help her avoid impulsive eating. Upon returning to her desk, she gives herself two minutes of silence to refocus her mind. Finally, at the end of the day, she closes with a brief review of her emotional state and a note of gratitude toward at least one person with whom she interacted positively.

This seemingly modest set of actions accumulates into an emotional resilience that makes it possible to maintain a demanding work pace without sacrificing personal well-being.

From then on, Claudia observes that her leadership ability improves, not through extraordinary techniques, but through the clarity that emanates from a rested body, a mind nourished with resources, and a support network that thrives on genuine conversations.

CONCLUSION

The final reflection on this topic invites us to view self-care as a fundamental investment. It's not a to-do list, but a way of being in the world: attentive to one's own needs, humble enough to ask for help when necessary, and courageous enough to design a life that sustains inner peace amidst a dynamic environment.

Recovering and maintaining this peace requires, first and foremost, recognizing vulnerability as a human condition, not a weakness. From this acceptance, people can create habits that nurture their emotional resilience and allow them to maintain healthy boundaries without losing connection with others. As each person takes care of themselves, their entire life benefits: there is more energy for relationships, responsibilities, and moments of rest that regenerate creativity and hope.

This chapter, then, proposes a practical and compassionate approach to self-care, a realistic path for peace of mind to take root in daily life and translate into a fuller, clearer, and more humane existence.

EIGHT
CULTIVATING GRATITUDE

Gratitude is not a mere gesture of courtesy or a ploy to feel good for a moment: it is a practice that transforms our attention and, consequently, the way we live each day. In this chapter, we explore daily gratitude practices as simple and sustainable tools for cultivating inner peace.

Gratitude, understood as the conscious recognition of what we already have, shifts our focus from what we lack to what we possess, and in this relocation of attention, an emotional stability emerges that becomes more resilient to the ups and downs of daily life. By cultivating this grateful perspective, we strengthen relationships, nurture a more compassionate view of ourselves and others, and open an inner space where calm can flourish even when life demands much of us.

Practicing daily gratitude doesn't require great sacrifices or complex rituals. It simply involves incorporating simple routines that, over time, become personalized and almost automatic.

One of the key suggestions is keeping a short gratitude journal: each day, dedicate a few minutes to writing down three things you are grateful for, along with a brief reflection on why that experience was meaningful.

This exercise isn't about accumulating an endless list of favors; it's about building an active memory that reinforces the feeling that life offers support and moments that deserve recognition.

In practice, this record functions as a kind of emotional map: it highlights which aspects of the day resonated with our needs, which small victories went unnoticed, and which people or circumstances deserve acknowledgment. With repetition, the gratitude journal becomes an internal resource that fosters resilience, reminding us that there are positive elements even in challenging situations.

Another key dimension is the recognition and explicit expression of gratitude towards others. Instead of simply feeling gratitude silently, this habit encourages genuinely communicating that recognition.

A brief message to a colleague for their support on a task, a note of appreciation for a family member who did something thoughtful, or a gesture of recognition towards a leader who guided the team through difficult times, are actions that strengthen relationships and elevate the emotional tone of the entire interaction.

This gesture not only benefits the recipient but also the giver: gratitude, when expressed, reinforces self-esteem, reduces rumination, and creates a climate of trust that facilitates cooperation and mutual care.

These exchanges, simple in their execution, generate a current of positivity that has a cumulative effect: throughout the week and the month, it translates into a network of stronger connections and a broader perception that everyday life is full of reasons to be grateful.

A third pillar of these practices is paying attention to the opportunities for gratitude that arise amidst difficulties. Gratitude doesn't mean ignoring tensions or challenges; on the contrary, it proposes noticing the positive even when circumstances aren't ideal.

For example, in a tense meeting, it's possible to be grateful for the learning the experience offers: the opportunity to practice listening, to clarify ideas, to identify what can be controlled, and to refine the action plan based on what has been learned. This approach doesn't minimize the reality of obstacles, but rather places them within a narrative that facilitates effective action.

When lessons and available resources are recognized, the mind focuses on solutions rather than endless complaints, and the energy previously spent complaining is channeled into more serene and productive execution.

The simplicity of these practices is their greatest strength. They don't require a mentor, a course, or a radical lifestyle change. They can be adopted in any context: at home, at work, during a commute, or during a break between activities. What's important is regularity and intention: each day, before diving into the day's activities, or at the end of it, dedicate a brief moment to acknowledging the positive. While gratitude may seem minor in the face of major challenges, its cumulative effect is profound.

Over time, this habitual practice becomes an emotional compass that guides decisions, manages emotions, and improves the quality of interactions with others. It's a process of inner strengthening that doesn't demand sacrifices, but rather a reconfiguration of what is valued and how that value is communicated to others.

A practical example to illustrate this idea: Imagine Laura, a project designer experiencing high-demand days and constant changes. Laura starts each day with a short note in her notebook: three things she's grateful for that morning, such as her team's support, the clarity of an instruction she received, or simply having a coffee to help her start calmly.

Midday, she sends a quick message to a colleague to acknowledge their contribution to a recent task, which strengthens collaboration and boosts the team's energy. At the end of the day, she writes a final entry in her gratitude journal, adding an observation about an interaction where she was able to listen attentively and respond with empathy, rather than react impulsively.

On difficult days, Laura reminds herself that gratitude doesn't erase the pressures, but it does shift the frame of reference from which she approaches situations: from complaining to learning, from hopelessness to the possibility of growth.

This small set of daily habits, repeated consistently, transforms gratitude into a practice that sustains clarity and serenity, even when the environment is uncooperative.

Gratitude, understood as a habit, is also linked to other components of healthy mental peace. When we cultivate a grateful outlook, we strengthen self-compassion and empathy, which in turn facilitates healthier boundaries and more balanced relationships.

A virtuous cycle is thus established: gratitude cultivates confidence and well-being, and this well-being reduces reactivity to stress, fostering a more deliberate response to everyday situations. Another less obvious but significant benefit is the building of an emotional memory that promotes a long-term perspective.

In moments of uncertainty or exhaustion, recalling past experiences of gratitude can activate a reservoir of hope and motivation to persevere, even when goals seem distant.

Finally, it is helpful to remember that gratitude is not a denial of difficulties nor a mask of forced optimism. Rather, it is a practice that acknowledges the complexity of life and yet chooses to emphasize what nourishes it:

- Connection with others,
- Acts of kindness received,
- Given, and the opportunity to learn from every experience.

Practical approaches to integrating these practices into daily life are varied and simple. You can start with a brief two- to five-minute morning ritual to quietly list three things you are grateful for in the day ahead. Then, throughout the day, make a small gesture of appreciation toward someone, either verbally or with a short message.

At the end of the day, take a few minutes to reflect on situations that challenged your serenity and note at least one lesson learned or action you can take next time. If you find it helpful, set a daily reminder to pause and give thanks, without relying on an external event.

Over time, these actions not only cultivate a more stable emotional state but also strengthen your ability to sustain mindfulness, patience, and empathy—core values for living with greater calm and clarity.

The final reflection on Daily Gratitude Practices invites us to see gratitude as a gentle yet powerful discipline. It's not about escaping reality, nor about a biased evaluation of life; it's about training ourselves to appreciate what is already present and to communicate that appreciation in a way that strengthens others and ourselves.

When gratitude becomes a habit, it transforms into a kind of emotional compass that guides decisions, relationships, and actions toward a more conscious and sustainable lifestyle. if this approach resonates with you, remember there are no shortcuts:

Consistency and authenticity are key.

Start today with a short journal entry, send yourself a message of appreciation, and allow the day to reveal to you, through the everyday, the richness of what you already have. In this way, gratitude ceases to be an add-on and becomes a stabilizing force that accompanies every step of your journey toward a more grounded and present peace of mind.

> Gratitude, when it becomes a daily practice, is not an emotional accessory; it is a way of focusing attention on what already exists and recognizing the value of interactions, small achievements, and the opportunities that unfold each day.

In this chapter, which continues the exploration begun in the previous topic, gratitude is addressed as a practical resource for sustaining inner peace amidst the demands of modern life. It is not a fleeting emotion in the face of adversity, but a sustained attitude that transforms how we perceive reality, relationships, and our own capabilities.

Integrating gratitude into daily life requires, above all, consistency and creativity: two qualities that allow an internal experience to translate into visible habits and concrete actions that benefit both ourselves and others.

The practice of gratitude doesn't deny difficulties; it places them within a framework of reflection and learning.

By cultivating a perspective that seeks the positive without denying complexity, a channel for emotional stability opens up, fostering clarity.

As the day presents challenges, gratitude acts as an anchor, reminding us of what is undeniably valuable: the opportunity to learn, connections with significant people, and the capacity to choose responses aligned with our values.

This approach isn't based on denying reality, but rather on the ability to distinguish between what is within our control and what is not, and, above all, on the decision to respond with appreciation instead of complaint.

To make gratitude a solid habit, it's helpful to break it down into simple, replicable practices. A clear path is implementing daily routines that don't require hours, but rather consistent minutes. One of the most useful tools is a gratitude journal, a brief record where you jot down three things you're grateful for each day. These three things don't have to be extraordinary; they can be everyday gestures, supportive gestures from a colleague, the feeling of having an object that makes a task easier, or simply overcoming a minor difficulty.

It's essential, however, to accompany this record with an attitude of observation: recognizing why these things matter, what need each one satisfies, and what actions could reinforce that feeling the next day. In this way, the journal doesn't become a list of achievements, but rather a map of feelings and connections that sustain emotional stability when the noise of daily life intensifies.

Another powerful approach is explicit recognition of others. Sending brief messages of appreciation, acknowledging a colleague's effort, or thanking someone for a simple gesture strengthens bonds and creates an atmosphere of reciprocity and support. These gestures of gratitude don't require grand gestures; they can be simple words, a short note in a chat, or a call to express appreciation.

The key is consistency: making recognition a daily practice that is repeated naturally, without forcing the situation or turning it into a rigid obligation. Over time, these actions fuel a "current" of positivity that reaches others and reinforces one's own well-being. The reader can imagine, for example, a brief exchange in which someone acknowledges the dedication of a teammate, not to praise them generically, but to highlight a specific contribution and its impact on the overall result.

This type of recognition has a multiplier effect: it reinforces helpful behaviors, boosts the self-esteem of the person receiving the recognition, and fosters shared responsibility.

Gratitude also manifests itself in the attention we pay to the qualities of others and the opportunities that arise. Noticing and appreciating the kindness of an act, the patience shown by someone in a tense situation, or the clarity with which a colleague resolved a problem are experiences that strengthen trust in relationships and in ourselves.

This attention is not naive; it is a conscious discernment of what adds value to daily life and a deliberate decision to reinforce what deserves to be nurtured. Furthermore, gratitude can be integrated with other personal development practices, such as nightly reflection or self-care routines, so that positive experiences become a source of sustained energy that supports decisions and actions the following day.

Creativity also plays a role in this framework. Not everyone responds to gratitude in the same way, and that's perfectly fine. Some find gratitude most effective when accompanied by practical gestures: returning favors, offering quality time to someone close, or transforming a thought into a concrete action that benefits others. Others may prefer to express gratitude through acts of service or tangible contributions to collective projects.

The key is to adapt these practices to one's personal circumstances, relationships, and daily responsibilities. In this sense, gratitude ceases to be a passive emotion and becomes a set of visible decisions that strengthen emotional resilience and the ability to remain calm amidst pressures.

A practical example of implementation could be the following. Marta, a professional who juggles multiple responsibilities, begins her day with a brief moment of gratitude, noting in her journal three things she appreciates about her work environment, such as a colleague's support, the opportunity to learn from a challenge, or a structure that facilitates her work.

During the day, she sends a short message to someone she worked with, highlighting a specific contribution and its impact on the project.

At lunch, she takes a minute to thank her team for their collaboration and acknowledge the collective effort. In the afternoon, she sets aside a few minutes to reflect on challenging situations and asks herself what those experiences taught her, recording a specific lesson and an action she can repeat tomorrow.

At the end of the day, she reviews her gratitude journal and adds a recent achievement related to a relationship with someone, strengthening the bond and her sense of personal progress. This seemingly modest routine can become a solid foundation for inner peace, as gratitude becomes a compass that guides her decisions, relationships, and responses to daily stress.

Gratitude, therefore, is not limited to an internal experience but manifests itself in habits that strengthen self-esteem, relationships, and the ability to cope with adversity. Over time, the regular practice of gratitude becomes an emotional infrastructure that facilitates decision-making in difficult times and reduces reactivity to stressful situations.

This chapter, then, proposes a clear vision: gratitude should be integrated as a natural element of life, a way of being that sustains serenity and clarity even when the environment demands speed, precision, and commitment.

Gratitude, when it becomes a habit, aligns with other practices in the book, such as self-care, stress management, and mindfulness, to sustain an inner peace that transcends fluctuating circumstances.

CONCLUSION

The final reflection invites us to see gratitude as a gentle yet powerful discipline that, through repetition, becomes internalized and integrated into daily life.

It is not an end in itself, but a means to sustain presence, foster empathy, and strengthen self-awareness.

The practices described—gratitude journaling, mindful recognition, and transforming gratitude into concrete actions—offer a path that can be adapted to any pace of life. Those who adopt this path discover that gratitude not only improves their momentary emotional state but also cultivates a predisposition to respond more coherently to what truly matters.

In the next section, we will connect these gratitude practices with emotional resilience, showing how a grateful heart and a clear mind create a more robust foundation for facing adversity without losing composure or our inner compass.

Gratitude, then, is not a fleeting spark, but a continuous practice that accompanies every decision, every interaction, and every step toward a more stable and meaningful life.

NINE
EMOTIONAL RESILIENCE

Emotional resilience is the ability to navigate adversity without losing your inner compass and, even more importantly, to extract learning and growth from each difficult experience. It's not about denying pain or finding an easy way out; it's about maintaining enough serenity to observe what is happening, respond with intention, and, from that impulse, strengthen confidence in your own coping abilities.

This chapter proposes viewing resilience as a set of practices and habits that strengthen the mind, body, and relationships, so that each challenge becomes an opportunity to cultivate calm and clarity. This perspective builds upon the foundations explored previously: self-knowledge, stress management, mindfulness, and the importance of boundaries and self-care as pillars of inner peace.

Emotional resilience is not an isolated trait; it is the result of continuous practice that integrates restorative sleep, conscious emotional hygiene, self-care routines, breathing exercises to stabilize anxiety, and a support network that accompanies you through stormy times.

Understanding it this way helps us understand why some fall, dust themselves off, and persevere, while others remain trapped in the noise of anxiety or despair.

Resilience, then, emerges as an active capacity: it is not the absence of difficulty, but the ability to maintain presence, to keep actions aligned with values, and to return the mind to a state where decisions are of higher quality.

In its essential dimension, emotional resilience involves a process of crisis reassessment: when an unexpected event occurs, the first response should not be succumbing to fear, but rather pausing to distinguish between what is within one's control and what is not.

This subtle yet powerful shift transforms the crisis into a learning experience. Reassessment consists of observing the situation with fresh eyes, questioning interpretations that magnify it, and seeking evidence of what is already working or could work in the future. By doing so, space is created to choose responses that are not driven by impulsiveness, but are anchored in a framework of reasoned action.

It is within this framework that breathing and emotional regulation play a fundamental role: simple breathing techniques, combined with gentle attention to bodily sensations, reduce physiological arousal and allow for the reconciliation of thoughts and emotions without one dominating the other.

In practical terms, conscious breathing, accompanied by brief pauses to refocus attention, becomes a support tool in the face of every emotional storm, from a tense meeting to unexpected news.

Seeking learning from adversity is another central element of resilience. Every crisis holds a lesson, and that lesson only emerges when we adopt an attitude of curiosity and responsibility.

This approach doesn't minimize the pain or complexity of situations; rather, it recognizes that growth doesn't happen by chance, but through the interplay of experience, reflection, and action. Journaling, end-of-day reflections, and regular reviews of our responses allow us to record triggers, thought patterns, and strategies that proved effective. Over time, this record transforms into a practical map for facing future challenges: warning signs are identified, possible responses are anticipated, and the ability to choose what truly brings clarity and well-being is refined.

A support network is another crucial pillar. Resilience is not an island; it thrives on human connections that offer listening, empathy, information, and practical help when demands increase. Expressing vulnerability at the right time is not a sign of weakness, but of emotional intelligence.

Asking for help when needed, facilitating honest conversations about boundaries and challenges, and maintaining reciprocity in relationships strengthen not only individual coping skills but also the quality of interactions with others.

This social support can come from friends, colleagues, family members, mentors, or communities that share values and self-care practices. In short, resilience flourishes when a support network is assembled that not only sustains us through crises but also enriches daily life with confidence and purpose.

Among the habits that strengthen emotional stability, adequate sleep and emotional hygiene stand out, establishing a foundation for other efforts to take effect. Sleep is not a luxury, but a necessity for memory, emotional regulation, and the energy needed to face the next day with the necessary focus.

Emotional hygiene involves simple and consistent practices for maintaining mental health: recognizing and naming emotions as they arise, allowing their expression without judgment, and adapting coping strategies according to the intensity of each moment. Self-care, understood as a set of actions that care for the body and mind, strengthens resilience against fatigue, irritability, and overload.

long these lines, breathing techniques, mindful pauses throughout the day, small self-care routines, and moments of rest are tools that, when repeated consistently, reduce reactivity and increase the ability to remain focused in the face of adversity.

Resilience also thrives on a conscious relationship with one's emotional environment. Practicing acceptance of what cannot be changed, without resignation, frees up energy to focus on what is within one's control: decisions, actions, and responses. This acceptance, along with attention to the present, reduces the tendency towards catastrophic thinking and strengthens a sense of control that is not contrived, but realistic.

In practice, this translates into brief reviews of decisions made in the face of adversity, an evaluation of results, and a willingness to adjust plans when circumstances demand it. Resilience, in this sense, does not seek an invulnerable end, but rather a continuity capable of sustaining serenity throughout life's inevitable changes: changes in work, relationships, health, or responsibilities.

This chapter also encourages us to consider resilience as a muscle that is strengthened with intention, not mere passive resistance.

The key lies in transforming acquired knowledge into habits that take root in daily life: brief check-ins to gauge emotional state and energy; routines that promote calm and clarity; and the ability to redirect course when signs of strain appear.

This practical approach connects with the themes covered in previous chapters:

The practice of self-awareness to understand what triggers emotions; stress management techniques to reduce the intensity of responses; and the discipline of mindfulness to maintain presence even amidst the noise.

Together, these tools allow us to sustain inner peace when external winds blow, without having to relinquish goals, responsibilities, or relationships. Emotional resilience, understood in this way, facilitates a more authentic and meaningful life, in which the ability to recover is not a passive consolation, but a proactive force that guides decisions, nurtures relationships, and keeps purpose alive.

Looking to the immediate future within the work, resilience is proposed as a foundation that will connect closely with the next theme: setting boundaries and self-care. The ability to face adversity calmly is strengthened when accompanied by clear boundaries that protect energy and time, and by self-care practices that support clarity of judgment and empathy.

Thus, resilience is not an isolated exception, but a central axis that supports and is nourished by other core principles of the book: self-awareness, stress management, mindfulness, and gratitude. With this integrated perspective, the reader can navigate life's challenges with greater emotional stability, without sacrificing openness to learning, caring, and relating to others from a more compassionate and effective standpoint.

Ultimately, emotional resilience is a life practice: a conscious discipline that transforms the way we respond to the world, strengthening inner calm and expanding the capacity to live with purpose, even when everything seems to demand a rapid reaction. Facing challenges without losing inner peace isn't a trick to avoid reality, but a discipline that transforms how we respond to what life throws our way.

This topic offers a range of strategies for managing emotions under pressure, developing alternative plans when circumstances change, and maintaining a curious attitude toward the unknown. The central idea is that inner peace doesn't depend on everything going as planned, but on the ability to stay grounded while the environment shifts.

Thus, the constellation of practices we've built throughout this book—self-awareness, stress management, mindfulness, and healthy boundaries—integrates into a broader response to adversity: a response that is deliberate, flexible, and sustained by simple yet powerful habits.

In developing these strategies, it is crucial to distinguish between the impulse to react at the first sign of tension and the ability to respond intentionally. Emotional modulation begins with a brief pause that may even seem insignificant, but which acts as an anchor: conscious breathing, a gentle glance at the surroundings, and a quick review of priorities.

This pause does not deny the emotion that arises; it acknowledges it and places it within a framework where the mind can evaluate options without the emotion governing action. From there, three complementary movements unfold: managing emotions, planning alternatives, and strategic curiosity in the face of the unknown. Emotional management involves identifying which emotion arises, what its function is, and what underlying need it is signaling.

Instead of allowing fear, frustration, or irritation to dictate behavior, the focus is on modulating its intensity and maintaining an inner voice that asks: "What do I need right now to decide clearly?"

This question opens space for responses based on values and objectives, rather than impulsive reactions that can worsen the situation. Alternative planning is the second key element: when a difficulty arises, instead of dwelling on the problem, at least two possible paths forward are generated.

This doesn't mean fantasizing about perfect solutions, but rather articulating realistic and actionable scenarios. For example, if a project faces an unforeseen delay from a supplier, the strategy involves mapping out options:

- Adjusting the schedule,
- Reallocating resources,
- Gathering additional information to renegotiate deadlines,
- Or activating a contingency plan through alternative suppliers.

Each option should be evaluated using practical criteria: impact on customer value, costs, risks, and time. The practice of developing these alternative plans, even quickly and conservatively, strengthens the sense of control and maintains composure, as the mind has verified paths at hand instead of being trapped in uncertainty.

Curiosity about the unknown acts as a driving force, transforming adversity into practical learning. When the situation is uncertain, curiosity prompts us to reframe questions:

What can I learn from this experience?

What signs indicate that I can adjust my approach without losing sight of my goals? Kind curiosity prevents us from falling into cynicism or denial, and fosters a broader understanding of reality.

This perspective facilitates the shift toward creative and realistic solutions because it asks about what we don't yet know and patiently observes what we do. Curiosity, understood in this way, becomes a source of energy that sustains proactive action even when circumstances are challenging.

These three dimensions don't work in isolation; they intertwine in a daily practice that can be summarized in simple, repeatable rituals. First, brief check-ins, which can occur at the beginning, middle, and end of the day. A morning check-in allows you to remember your values and goals; a brief midday check-in helps you assess whether the decisions you're making still reflect your priorities and real needs; a light check-in at the end of the day facilitates the transfer of learning to future action.

Second, mindful breathing and body awareness act as anchors that soften reactivity to sudden stress. A couple of minutes of diaphragmatic breathing or a conscious pause to notice signs of muscle tension can make the difference between continuing down a stress-driven path and stopping to readjust your course with clarity.

Third, gratitude and reviewing successes, however small, sustain motivation and confidence. Recognizing what works, what you've accomplished, and who you can thank strengthens your energy to face the next challenge.

The book has already shown that a support network is a critical component of emotional resilience. In this chapter, that network becomes more conscious and deliberate: recognizing when it is appropriate to ask for help, delegate tasks, or consult with colleagues or mentors to gain different perspectives.

Asking for help is not a sign of weakness, but a smart strategy to broaden one's resource base and reduce the burden of mental strain. When a person shares a challenge, it opens the possibility of co-responsibility, which lightens individual pressure and increases the likelihood of finding effective solutions.

Furthermore, the presence of others not only offers practical support, but also a mirror that helps identify biases, distortions, or beliefs that may be clouding decision-making. With this collaboration, the experience becomes richer, and the capacity to sustain inner peace is strengthened, as it is enriched by different perspectives and skills.

To illustrate these ideas, let's consider a specific situation. A team leader faces a crucial meeting where a colleague questions the feasibility of a proposed plan. Instead of reacting defensively or with frustration, she pauses briefly, takes a controlled breath, and observes her emotions with curiosity. She identifies the dominant emotion as uncertainty and a need for clarity.

Then, she implements an alternative plan: she presents data and examples to support the plan, proposes two timeline adjustments, and requests a brief follow-up review to validate the decisions with the team.

During the discussion, she asks openly, "What evidence would we need to move forward with confidence?" Meanwhile, she maintains a supportive attitude toward her colleague, thanks them for their concern, and acknowledges the value of the criticism in strengthening the project.

At the end of the meeting, she records in her journal the signs of stress, the beliefs that emerged, and the strategies that proved effective. This record is not just a memory, but a guide for future situations—a map that allows her to transform adverse experiences into practical, actionable learning.

CONCLUSION

The final reflection on this topic is simple yet powerful: inner peace in challenging times doesn't depend on the difficulty disappearing. It depends on the ability to regulate emotions, plan flexibly, and cultivate a curiosity that transforms uncertainty into fertile ground for action.

Each day offers a new opportunity to practice these skills; every practice, however small it may seem, strengthens the capacity to respond with clarity and courage. Emotional resilience thus emerges as a way of life that integrates self-care, sustainable productivity, quality relationships, and fairness to oneself in the face of the unknown.

If we maintain these principles in our daily practice, inner peace will not be a fleeting refuge, but a continuous state of presence, guided by empathy, evidence, and a willingness to learn.

TEN
MAINTAINING LONG-TERM PEACE OF MIND

Maintaining long-term peace of mind is not a static state achieved once and for all; it is, above all, a sustained practice integrated into daily life. This chapter proposes a clear roadmap of steps and habits that can sustain clarity, empathy, and curiosity throughout the different stages of life.

The central idea is simple and powerful: inner peace that withstands wear and tear doesn't depend on changing everything at once, but rather on creating a framework of simple, repeatable habits that, over time, become natural and reliable. In this framework, three principles act as compasses: regularity, flexibility, and connection to what truly matters. Daily practice, understood as a series of small but consistent actions, ensures that peace of mind is not an isolated exception but a way of life that accompanies every decision, every interaction, and every moment of rest.

The foundation of emotional stability lies in sustainable habits that seamlessly integrate into our routines. These aren't extravagant rituals or extraordinary efforts, but rather subtle adjustments that become habitual over time. Previous chapters explored tools such as self-awareness, stress management, mindfulness, and respecting boundaries; here, they are brought together to show how they can work together as a life strategy.

When cultivated, these practices cease to feel like chores and begin to feel like conditions that allow us to respond with presence to daily complexity.

Thus, inner peace no longer depends on exceptional moments and becomes a quality that permeates from the first hours of the day until its end, even when circumstances become more demanding.

A practical structure for cultivating stability involves three key moments throughout the day:

- A wellness-focused start,
- A deliberate midday pause, and
- An end-of-day review that connects learning and action.

The brief and accessible morning ritual proposes dedicating five to ten minutes to a set of simple actions: drinking water, doing gentle stretches to awaken the body, and setting an intention for the day. This light and repeatable combination establishes a foundation of presence that extends throughout subsequent tasks. The one- to two-minute midday pause acts as an anchor for attention: activity stops, conscious breathing takes place, and bodily sensations and emerging emotions are observed.

In this brief moment, a conscious decision is made about how to proceed in a specific situation: responding clearly or adjusting the strategy as needed. In the afternoon or evening, a light review of the day, accompanied by a brief note on lessons learned or adjustments, closes the cycle and prepares the ground for the following day.

There are variations to suit different lifestyles: some people can extend their morning session to ten minutes; others, with particularly busy days, keep the sequence to a minimum, without losing the essence of presence. In any case, the central idea is to maintain regularity and avoid the temptation to turn inner peace into an impossible or unattainable goal.

Implementing sustainable habits isn't limited to the personal sphere; its impact multiplies when aligned with the environment and relationships. An environment that fosters calm facilitates the continuity of these practices: a quiet space at home or in the office, soft lighting, simple objects that remind us to respond with presence, and clear boundaries that protect moments of mindfulness.

Similarly, communicating needs and boundaries at work and in personal relationships should be clear and respectful, so that demands don't drain energy or fragment attention. This approach isn't about rigidity, but rather a way to maintain serenity in the face of the complexity of modern life.

Consistency between self-care practices, mindfulness, and healthy boundaries is key to ensuring that peace of mind doesn't depend on constantly changing external circumstances, but rather on an internal structure that remains stable despite environmental variations.

> Periodic goal review acts as a bridge between intention and sustained action. Instead of waiting for radical changes, it's a continuous process of adjustment that recognizes that goals can evolve as life does.

This simple and practical process involves reviewing personal and professional objectives weekly or bi-weekly, assessing progress, identifying recurring obstacles, and recording small achievements that fuel motivation.

Evidence of progress, however modest, strengthens confidence in one's ability to maintain inner peace. At the same time, goal review encourages readjusting commitments, delegating when necessary, and redirecting energy toward activities and people that nurture serenity.

This practice isn't an added burden; it becomes a learning tool and a way to align daily actions with one's deepest values and priorities. Life isn't linear, and therefore, flexibility emerges as a core skill.

Lasting peace of mind requires the ability to adapt habits without losing the essence of the practice.

Life stages, work responsibilities, family changes, or personal shifts may require adjustments to the routine.

The key lies in preserving the core structure—a framework of simple rituals and moments of pause—moments that, while modified in duration or focus, maintain continuity of attention and care.

This flexible approach allows the reader to maintain serenity without feeling constrained by external pressures. In this sense, consistency doesn't imply rigidity, but rather a conscious constancy that respects life's variations.

Gratitude, mindfulness, and self-awareness remain central resources in this chapter, not as isolated elements, but as threads that intertwine to sustain inner peace. Gratitude fosters emotional stability and resilience, reminding us that even in the face of challenges, there are valuable aspects that deserve recognition and care. Mindfulness, practiced daily, helps us maintain presence in every interaction and decision, preventing mental chatter from dominating our actions.

Self-awareness, for its part, strengthens our ability to accurately interpret internal signals and respond from a place of clarity and alignment with our values. When these tools work together, the result is a life in which peace of mind is consistently present at work, in relationships, and at rest, without depending on any fluctuating external circumstances.

To sustain this peace over time, it's helpful to remember three key ideas. First, consistency is more powerful than the length of a single session: ten minutes a day, repeated consistently, can generate more change than long, sporadic sessions. Second, acceptance is essential: setbacks are part of learning, not a defeat; each detour offers an opportunity to return to mindfulness with greater wisdom and self-compassion.

Third, gentle curiosity facilitates continuity: every experience, even distraction or frustration, becomes information that guides adjustments and improvements.

Within this framework, the reader is invited to envision a personal journey, in which each day contributes a modest but significant step toward a more conscious, empathetic, and stable life.

> The promise of this chapter is clear: lasting peace of mind is not a static refuge, but a way of relating to life that is strengthened by simple, repeatable, and adaptable habits.

By establishing self-care routines, mindfulness practices, clear boundaries, and a culture of gratitude and learning, each person can maintain calm even when the outside world moves quickly. This is a path that doesn't demand radical, all-out changes, but rather a patient and consistent focus on what is worth cultivating day after day.

If this focus is maintained, inner peace ceases to be a distant ideal and becomes an everyday experience, present in every decision, every interaction, and every moment of pause that allows for intentional choices.

In short, this chapter invites us to embrace the idea of peace of mind as a life project, not a specific goal. Stability stems from habits that breathe and are nourished by daily experience: self-care, being present in the here and now, the clarity to distinguish what depends on us and what doesn't, and the ability to respond purposefully to what life presents.

With this set of tools, inner peace becomes a constant guide that illuminates the path and sustains life in its complexity, with dignity, empathy, and an undying curiosity.

If you heed this call, the invitation is to design a personal continuity plan that combines simple practices, reminders, and rituals that align with your natural rhythm. Long-term peace of mind is not a miracle, but rather the result of faithfully focusing on what matters, a daily practice that adapts without losing its essence, and a commitment to your own well-being expressed through concrete actions and healthier relationships.

With this foundation, life can unfold with greater clarity, balance, and a presence that, step by step, solidifies as a way of being in the world.

This chapter offers a synthesis of what has been learned and a clear vision for the reader's immediate future: maintaining peace of mind over time, regardless of changing circumstances, through a personal plan that integrates simple habits, continuous mindfulness, and openness to learning.

This is not an exceptional talent reserved for a select few; it is a practical, human, and sustainable method that adapts to daily life. Throughout this journey, the reader has acquired tools for honest observation, stress management, constructive thinking, mindful presence, setting boundaries, and cultivating gratitude. Now it is time to transform this accumulated learning into a personal plan that sustains calm, clarity, and intentional action in every area of life.

Peace of mind, as it has been understood, is not a promise of the absence of difficulties. It is a state of being in relation to what happens, in which the mind learns to distinguish what depends on oneself from what does not, and to respond with intention instead of reacting impulsively.

This foundation does not change in the face of a crisis or a particularly exhausting day. What does change is the way life is organized to sustain this state of being.

This chapter proposes three key elements that have proven effective throughout the book:

Consistency in simple habits, patience to allow the response to mature, and curiosity to understand what each experience has to teach.

> Consistency, rather than requiring extraordinary effort, manifests itself in micro-habits that fit into the daily schedule without demanding radical sacrifices.

A recurring example is dedicating five to ten minutes to conscious breathing upon waking, adding brief pauses throughout the day to return attention to the body, and concluding with an emotional review at night to identify lessons learned and areas for improvement.

Patience, for its part, encourages us to trust in a gradual pace: sustained change takes time, and when allowed to unfold, it generates a serenity that withstands turbulence. And curiosity acts as a learning engine: every emotion, every thought, and every situation becomes an opportunity to better understand our needs, our beliefs, and how to respond in a way that is more aligned with our values.

Looking back, it's clear that each chapter of the book has contributed an essential piece to this vision of continuity. In Identifying Mental Obstacles, we learned to recognize triggers and automatic thoughts, to pause in the moment to record what happened, and to use simple tools like diaphragmatic breathing to reduce reactivity.

In Self-Awareness Techniques, we discovered the importance of listening to emotions with curiosity, mapping patterns, and maintaining a journaling practice to build an internal map that guides our decisions. Stress Management Strategies taught us how to incorporate mindful breathing, progressive relaxation, and short breaks into our daily routine, so that stress ceases to be a constant threat and becomes a manageable part of the day.

In the realm of Positive Thinking, we saw how restructuring thoughts, using evidence-based affirmations, and keeping a gratitude journal strengthen an internal narrative that fosters conscious action.

Mindfulness and Meditation offered a practical path to experiencing presence in everyday life, with short, adaptable sessions and a philosophy of acceptance that sustains attention despite distractions.

Setting Boundaries and Self-Care showed that caring for oneself is not selfishness, but a necessary condition for maintaining serenity in the face of external demands. Cultivating Gratitude transformed attention into a compass that guides relationships, decisions, and habits, and Emotional Resilience explained how a support network, restful sleep, and self-care routines strengthen the capacity to recover and learn.

All of this, united by the idea that inner peace is not a destination, but an ongoing practice, offers a solid roadmap for confidently moving toward maintaining calm.

To transform that map into a personal plan, it's helpful to think about a framework of habits that allows you to maintain peace of mind without depending on perfect conditions.

First, it's advisable to establish three daily rhythms that serve as anchors: a morning ritual that sets your intention, a brief pause midday to refocus your attention, and an evening review that transforms the experience into practical learning.

Second, it's key to design an environment that fosters clarity: a small sanctuary at home or in the office with soft lighting and an object that serves as a reminder of your intention to respond calmly. Third, the plan should include clear boundaries and self-care strategies that can be integrated without requiring a complete reorganization of your personal or professional schedule.

These routines aren't meant to eliminate stress, but rather to provide the mind with a safe framework to assess what's happening and consciously decide on the next action.

The daily narrative of this plan should include previously established tools that have proven effective. Mindful breathing and diaphragmatic breathing remain powerful anchors for returning to the present moment.

Mindful pauses of a minute or two allow you to pause before acting, evaluate options, and avoid impulsive responses. Journaling continues to be a valuable resource for recording triggers, beliefs, and effective responses, allowing you to see patterns over time and adjust strategies. Gratitude, practiced consistently, maintains motivation and strengthens connections with others, reinforcing an emotional foundation that supports resilience through ups and downs.

The personal plan must also consider the possibility of life changes. Lasting peace of mind requires flexibility: when new responsibilities arise, roles change, moves occur, or family dynamics shift, practices must be adaptable without losing their essence.

This adaptability is fundamental: it's not a rigid set of rules, but a living framework that molds itself to circumstances without abandoning its core purpose. The key is to stay true to your principles: presence, clarity, empathy, and values-based action. In this sense, continuity is not mere repetition, but the perpetuation of learning that translates into healthier decisions and relationships.

The case study used to illustrate this topic clearly demonstrates how this design can be applied in an everyday work scenario. A project manager faces a tense meeting. Before it begins, she takes a diaphragmatic breath to anchor her attention; she identifies the dominant emotion, typically anxiety about the uncertainty, and summarizes the objective facts without judgment. Based on this clarity, she proposes two concrete paths forward, each grounded in evidence, and requests a follow-up meeting to agree on the next step. During the meeting, she records in her journal the feelings, triggers, and responses that worked, so that this record can guide future interventions.

This example doesn't describe a magic bullet, but rather demonstrates that daily practice, when integrated into real life, generates more deliberate responses that are aligned with values and objectives. It is in this consistency that the strength of the plan lies: each day adds a layer of experience that strengthens the ability to remain calm, even when the environment pushes toward haste and pressure.

A final reflection invites us to see inner peace as a constellation of sustainable habits. The vision for the future proposed in this chapter is, above all, one of continuity and constant learning. It's about cultivating a growth mindset that sees each challenge as an opportunity to practice and solidify the principles already known: self-care, boundaries, gratitude, mindfulness, and stress management.

Daily practice shouldn't be a to-do list; it should become a way of being in the world, of responding calmly to adversity, and of maintaining clarity in all interactions.

Ultimately, lasting peace of mind emerges when the reader maintains an active commitment to life, intelligently adjusts their habits in the face of change, and continues to strengthen their capacity to listen, understand, and act in accordance with their deepest values.

This is the promise of the path presented in this chapter: not an abandonment of reality, but an increasingly wise relationship with it.

CONCLUSION

In closing, it's helpful to remember that the concepts that have accompanied this journey—peace of mind, mindful observation, diaphragmatic breathing, conscious responses, thought journaling, gratitude journaling, emotional hygiene, self-care routines, boundaries, and gratitude as a compass—are not merely concepts, but living tools that can be sustained over time.

Their gradual implementation, their integration into daily life, and their combination with an attitude of curiosity and empathy are the keys to maintaining inner peace, even when the outside world moves quickly. If the reader continues to apply these ideas with honesty and patience, calm ceases to be a distant state and becomes a way of living: present, compassionate, and capable of creating meaning even amidst challenges.

This is the purpose of Maintaining Long-Term Peace of Mind in its second installment: to guide the reader in the transition from occasional practice to a consistency that transforms, day after day, the experience of living.

AFTERWORD

What remains after closing these pages is not a magic formula, but a daily practice that transforms our relationship with life as it is. Healthy peace of mind doesn't come as a prize reserved for a select few, but as a way of being that is learned, nurtured, and sustained through small, consistent actions.

Along this journey, we have seen how clarity arises from self-awareness, how serenity is strengthened by acceptance, and how simple habits sustain the mind and body in the face of the world's acceleration. We have explored, in different tones and scenarios, that inner peace is not the absence of difficulty, but the capacity to respond with intention when reality demands something real, and at the same time, to maintain dignity in the face of discomfort.

The synthesis of this book can be read as a map of three interwoven planes: mastering our attention and emotions (self-awareness), the ability to moderate tension and stress (stress management and mindfulness), and the capacity to care for ourselves and the relationships that sustain life (boundaries, self-care, and gratitude).

From there, the stories and exercises showed that inner peace is nurtured by three pillars: the daily practice of observing without judgment, the acceptance that releases energy for action, and the commitment to habits that strengthen serenity, day after day.

This triangle, articulated with consistency, patience, and curiosity, creates a foundation that doesn't depend on external circumstances, but rather on a wiser relationship with what happens.

In practice, inner peace emerges when we transform ideas into visible habits. A few minutes of mindful breathing, a pause to reflect on a decision, a journal of thoughts or gratitude, a conversation that sets boundaries with empathy, a short walk that cultivates presence: these actions are repeated, refined, and cease to be extras, becoming the backbone of daily life.

What seemed demanding or unattainable at the start of the day transforms, with consistency, into a more stable experience, capable of supporting work, relationships, and rest without a single event shaking our inner foundation.

This book, then, proposes a personal design that each reader can adapt. Three moments of the day—beginning, pause, and end—serve as anchors to sustain presence.

A gentle environment, clear boundaries, and a support network are not embellishments, but rather catalysts for continuity.

Breathing and mindfulness cease to be isolated techniques and become a way of relating to reality; gratitude ceases to be an occasional gesture and becomes an emotional compass; resilience, strengthened by sleep, self-care, and honest conversation, becomes a practice that accompanies decisions and vulnerabilities.

Ultimately, inner peace rests on an architecture of habits that breathes, learns, and adapts to each stage of life.

Looking ahead, the invitation isn't to abandon theory for practice, but rather to make practice a natural part of each day. Designing a personal continuity plan means identifying which rituals work for you: five or ten minutes upon waking to set an intention, brief pauses to listen to your body and review priorities, and a nightly review that transforms the experience into learning.

It also means building an environment that reduces friction between intention and action: a calm corner, simple reminders, words that reiterate the difference between responding and reacting. And, above all, keeping the spirit of curiosity alive: every emotion, every thought, and every challenge is an opportunity to understand yourself better and to adjust your course with empathy and courage.

May this book serve as a companion, not a rigid rule. May the peace of mind it offers become a constant presence in every decision, every conversation, and every moment of rest. By cultivating consistency, patience, and curiosity, the mind will find its own rhythm, the will will find its direction, and the heart will find its purpose: to live with greater clarity, greater empathy, and increasingly conscious action.

This is not an ending, but an invitation to continue cultivating a life in which inner peace, far from being a whim, is the very way of being in the world.

FINAL WORDS

Dear reader, as I close this book, I want to thank you for joining me on this journey toward a more attainable, everyday peace of mind. If you have followed these chapters, you know that inner peace is not a static refuge, but a practice enriched by self-awareness, acceptance, and simple habits repeated with kindness. We have explored breath as an anchor, a thought journal as a map, self-talk as a guide, and gratitude as a compass; we have remembered that boundaries and self-care sustain serenity even when the world presses.

This closure doesn't promise a definitive solution, but rather inaugurates a commitment: to freely design a personal continuity plan that adapts to each stage of life. I invite you to transform these ideas into daily micro-actions: a pause, a note, a values-based decision.

Share your findings or challenges if you wish; inner peace also flourishes through conversation and mutual support.

I wish you peace of mind as a constant presence in your daily life, at the office, at home, in every encounter. May every choice be made with intention, and may curiosity continue to illuminate your path. Thank you for trusting this book to accompany your growth.

ABOUT THE AUTHOR

Luis Fernando Rodrigo Vallebona is a businessman, entrepreneur, and self-taught author. At the age of twelve, he began forging his own path through what he calls the true university of life—a lifelong education built on hard work, sacrifice, mistakes, perseverance, and an unwavering determination to move forward. Without privilege or clear guidance, he learned early on that the only way to stand out was through consistency, discipline, and resilience.

His books are not born from theory but from lived experience. Through them, he shares reflections shaped by setbacks, personal rebuilding, and the conviction that every obstacle can become an opportunity for growth. Rather than teaching from a position of authority, his goal is to inspire those facing adversity to regain confidence in themselves, transform failure into wisdom, and move forward through purposeful action toward a meaningful life.

Convinced that true progress is built one day at a time, he uses the metaphor of the train to remind readers that every stage of life is a station where decisions shape destiny and leave a lasting legacy.

As a son, husband, father of four, and passionate advocate for personal growth, he hopes each of his books will ignite the spark of change in those determined to rise again, persevere, and build a legacy that endures.

THANK YOU FOR READING

DEAR READER,

Thank you for accompanying me on this journey through these pages. If this book resonated with you, inspired you, or offered some light on your path, I invite you to leave a review where you purchased it.

Your words are a beacon that helps other seekers find this message, and they mean more than you can imagine.

Thank you from the heart for your support and for being part of this journey.

APPENDIX

This appendix compiles the sources and editorial references that support the ideas and practices presented throughout *Healthy Mental Peace*, highlighting foundational texts on mindfulness, emotional management, and personal growth. These references are offered as a guide for further reading and verification of key concepts, not intended to replace the lived experience of daily practice.

- Jon Kabat-Zinn, Wherever You Go, There You Are.
- Jon Kabat-Zinn, Mindfulness for Beginners.
- Thich Nhat Hanh, The Miracle of Mindfulness.
- Thich Nhat Hanh, No Mud, No Lotus.
- Kristin Neff, Self-Compassion.
- Rick Hanson, Buddha's Brain.
- Tara Brach, Radical Acceptance.
- Daniel Goleman, Emotional Intelligence.

- Susan David, Emotional Agility.
- Stephen Porges, The Polyvagal Theory.
- Brené Brown, Daring Greatly.
- Daniell Goleman, Focus: The Hidden Driver of Excellence. (plausible editorial note to expand ties between focus and calm; moderate use)

These works and concepts provide the theoretical and practical framework that supports the self-care practices, mindfulness, thought restructuring, and resilience strengthening described in the book, and can serve as supplementary readings for readers who wish to delve deeper into breathing techniques, emotional regulation, and sustainable habits throughout daily life.

GLOSSARY OF TERMS

Peace of mind: It is the constant relationship with life from a center of clarity and calm. It does not imply the absence of problems, but rather the ability to respond intentionally to them, maintaining emotional stability and focus on values and goals.

Self-awareness: The ability to observe one's own reactions, thoughts, and sensations without judgment. It functions as an internal compass to identify triggers and decide on actions more aligned with well-being.

Acceptance: Allowing emotions and thoughts to arise as they are, without forcing immediate solutions. It reduces resistance and creates space to act with clarity and purpose.

Healthy habits: Simple and sustainable routines that keep mind and body in balance. Their daily practice accumulates benefits that strengthen emotional regulation and the capacity for conscious action.

Diaphragmatic breathing: A deep breathing technique that expands the abdomen to activate the parasympathetic nervous system. It facilitates muscle relaxation and reduces reactivity to stress.

Mindfulness: A conscious relationship with the present moment, observing thoughts, emotions, and sensations without judgment. It develops clarity, patience, and the ability to respond rather than react.

Conscious pause: A brief, deliberate interruption to evaluate possible responses before acting. It serves as an anchor to regain clarity and align action with values.

Thought journal: A brief record of facts, emotions, and beliefs that emerge in key situations. It helps identify patterns and guide more effective interventions.

Gratitude journal: Practice writing down three things you are grateful for and why they matter. It strengthens emotional resilience and improves relationships.

Journaling: A writing activity used to process internal experiences and map patterns. It complements other self-awareness and decision-making practices.

Restructuring thoughts: The process of identifying limiting beliefs, evaluating evidence, and formulating more realistic interpretations. It facilitates evidence-based decisions and reduces anxiety.

Triggers: Signals or situations that activate stress or anxiety responses. Recognizing them allows intervention before they take over.

Automatic thoughts: Quick and abrupt beliefs that arise in response to a stimulus and are often biased. They are subject to questioning and re-evaluation.

Emotional hygiene: Practices for maintaining mental health, such as recognizing emotions, expressing them freely, and adapting coping strategies. It's a daily practice.

Self-care: A set of actions to care for the body and mind, allowing one to maintain energy, empathy, and performance. It is the foundation for stable inner peace.

Boundaries: Clear boundaries that protect energy, time, and priorities. They communicate needs and facilitate sustainable and respectful collaborations.

Assertive communication: Honest expression of needs and boundaries with respect for others. It balances one's own rights and those of others to reduce conflict.

Support network: A group of people who offer listening, guidance, and practical help. It strengthens resilience and facilitates action in the face of adversity.

Emotional resilience: The ability to recover and learn from adversity while maintaining calm and focus. It is strengthened through healthy habits, a support network, and constant reflection.

RESOURCES AND REFERENCES

Below is a curated selection of resources, tools, and practical approaches that expand upon and strengthen the path outlined in Healthy Mental Peace, enabling the reader to bring these ideas into daily life with continuity and meaning.

- Diaphragmatic breathing and nervous system regulation. Practicing deep, conscious breathing helps activate the pause between stimulus and action, reducing hypervigilance and facilitating clearer decisions in stressful situations. Useful as an anchor in any context, from the office to home.
- Mindful pauses and micro-routines. Incorporating brief intervals of mindfulness throughout the day—a minute of breathing, a relaxing count, or a quick intention check—generates a cumulative change in the quality of responses and mental clarity.

- Thought journal and trigger log. Keeping a short record of situations, feelings, and thoughts allows you to map patterns, anticipate triggers, and choose more deliberate responses. Over time, the journal becomes a practical guide for intervening before emotions escalate.
- Thought restructuring techniques. Identifying automatic beliefs, contrasting them with evidence, and reformulating more realistic interpretations offers a concrete path to reducing rumination and sustaining optimism grounded in reality.
- Gratitude and appreciation journal. Writing down three things you are grateful for and expressing appreciation to others strengthens emotional resilience, improves relationships, and fosters a more constructive view of circumstances.
- Mindfulness and brief meditations. Short, consistent sessions allow you to experience presence, acceptance, and the separation between stimulus and response—key tools for maintaining calm in everyday life.
- Evening review and learning reading. A daily wrap-up that synthesizes learning, identifies adjustments, and reinforces a plan for the next day transforms the experience into continuous growth.
- Setting boundaries and self-care. Practicing assertive communication, managing expectations, and distributing responsibilities protects energy

and maintains clarity of thought, especially in work and family environments.

- Self-care routines: rest, mindful eating, movement, creativity, and social connection. These five areas support energy, memory, and emotional regulation, allowing us to act with greater presence and empathy.
- Progressive muscle relaxation and visualization of calm. Quick techniques to deactivate physical and mental tension, complementary to breathing, which strengthen the ability to sustain attention and working memory.
- A network of support and conscious coexistence. Asking for help, delegating, and seeking diverse perspectives enrich decision-making and strengthen collective resilience in the face of difficulties.
- Personal continuity plan. Design, adapt, and periodically review a plan of simple habits, rituals to begin and end the day, and adjustment strategies to cope with changes, to sustain inner peace over time.
- Supplementary readings and personal development exercises. Explore materials that expand your understanding of self-awareness, gratitude, empathy, and emotional management, supporting a path of continuous learning.

These resources, described from the perspective of everyday practice, encourage integration, adaptation, and experimentation. The key is consistency and an openness to learning from each experience, so that peace of mind remains a stable, useful, and human presence in every aspect of life.